WHAT YOUR COLLEAGUES ARE SAYING . . .

Thomas R. Guskey has done it again! *Engaging Parents and Families in Grading Reforms* is a must-read for educators seeking to transform their grading systems in a successful way. Drawing from a myriad of practical insights and real-world examples, Dr. Guskey offers real and actionable strategies that empower educators to navigate the complexities of grading reform successfully. It underscores the vital role of involving parents and families in the process, making it an imperative resource for anyone committed to improving education.

—Garth Larson
Co-Founder and CEO
FIRST Educational Resources
Oshkosh, WI

Thomas R. Guskey has been an instrumental partner in the reform of the Bethlehem Area School District's assessment and grading system. His evidence-based approaches and practical strategies to inform and engage parents have been important factors in our successful transformation. Dr. Guskey shows how parents can, and should, be key supporters of improved grading and reporting systems.

—Jack P. Silva
Superintendent of Schools
Bethlehem Area School District
Bethlehem, PA

Engaging Parents and Families in Grading Reforms guides educators on becoming true partners with parents and families in education and describes how educators can best support parents' understanding of purposeful grading. Thomas R. Guskey is one of education's best when it comes to sharing effective grading practices and strategies that support students and their learning.

—Jensen Ball
Consultant & Manager
Hawaii State Department of Education
Honolulu, HI

T0368829

When it comes to educational change, we have tended to focus on teachers and students. While this makes sense, it has left parents and families on the outside looking in. They want to understand the changes we're making but haven't been included in the conversation. Parents need a compass, direction, and understanding as to what we're up to. They don't need an atlas to figure out what we're doing—they need only a map. With this book, Thomas R. Guskey has supplied precisely that.

—Myron Dueck
Vice-Principal for Communicating Student Learning
Okanagan Skaha School District No. 67
Penticton, British Columbia

When I read *Engaging Parents and Families in Grading Reforms*, my first thought was "Why did I not read this sooner?" Having both led (or attempted to lead) grading reform in schools and studied the change experiences of school stakeholders, I am thrilled to finally find this straightforward, practical, and relevant guide that informs crucial shifts to the way leaders approach the change process with families. Without question, Guskey's newest book should be required reading for educators who have ever endeavored to lead meaningful change in grading practices for an entire community.

—Lindsay Prendergast
School Improvement Coach
NWEA
Portland, OR
lindspren@gmail.com

ENGAGING PARENTS AND FAMILIES IN GRADING REFORMS

Thomas R. Guskey

FOR INFORMATION:

Corwin

A SAGE Company

2455 Teller Road

Thousand Oaks, California 91320

(800) 233-9936

www.corwin.com

SAGE Publications Ltd.

1 Oliver's Yard

55 City Road

London EC1Y 1SP

United Kingdom

SAGE Publications India Pvt. Ltd.

Unit No 323-333, Third Floor, F-Block

International Trade Tower Nehru Place

New Delhi 110 019

India

SAGE Publications Asia-Pacific Pte.Ltd.

18 Cross Street #10-10/11/12

China Square Central

Singapore 048423

Vice President and Editorial
  Director: Monica Eckman

Program Director and Publisher: Dan Alpert

Acquisitions Editor: Megan Bedell

Content Development Editor: Mia Rodriguez

Senior Editorial Assistant: Natalie Delpino

Project Editor: Amy Schroller

Copy Editor: Shannon Kelly

Typesetter: C&M Digitals (P) Ltd.

Cover Designer: Candice Harman

Marketing Manager: Melissa Duclos

Library of Congress Cataloging-in-Publication Data

Names: Guskey, Thomas R., author.

Title: Engaging parents and families in grading reforms / Thomas R. Guskey.

Description: Thousand Oaks, California : Corwin, [2024] | Includes bibliographical references and index.

Identifiers: LCCN 2023046557 | ISBN 9781071921289 (paperback : acid-free paper) | ISBN 9781071921296 (epub) | ISBN 9781071921302 (epub) | ISBN 9781071921319 (pdf)

Subjects: LCSH: Education—Parent participation—United States. | Report cards—United States. | Grading and marking (Students)—United States. | Feedback (Psychology) | Communication in education—Social aspects—United States. | Parent-teacher relationships—United States. | Home and school—United States.

Classification: LCC LB1048.5 .G87 2024 | DDC 371.19/2—dc23/eng/20231103
LC record available at https://lccn.loc.gov/2023046557

CONTENTS

ABOUT THE AUTHOR

Thomas R. Guskey, PhD, is Professor Emeritus in the College of Education at the University of Kentucky. A graduate of the University of Chicago's renowned Measurement, Evaluation, and Statistical Analysis (MESA) program, he began his career in education as a middle school teacher, served as an administrator in the Chicago Public Schools, and was the first director of the Center for the Improvement of Teaching and Learning, a national educational research center. He is the author/editor of twenty-seven books and over three hundred articles published in prominent research journals as well as for *Educational Leadership*, *Kappan*, and *The School Administrator*.

Dr. Guskey served on the Policy Research Team of the National Commission on Teaching and America's Future and on the task force to develop the National Standards for Professional Development. He was named a Fellow in the American Educational Research Association and was awarded the association's prestigious Relating Research to Practice Award. He was also awarded Learning Forward's Outstanding Contribution to the Field Award and Phi Delta Kappan's Distinguished Educator Award. Perhaps most unique, in the 158-year history of his undergraduate institution, Thiel College, he is one of only three graduates to receive the Outstanding Alumnus Award and be inducted into the Thiel College Athletic Hall of Fame.

His most recent books include *Implementing Mastery Learning* (2023), *Instructional Feedback: The Power, the Promise, the Practice* (with Smith &

Lipnevich, 2023); *Get Set, Go! Creating Successful Grading and Reporting Systems* (2020), *What We Know about Grading* (with Brookhart, 2019), and *On Your Mark: Challenging the Conventions of Grading and Reporting* (2015). He may be contacted by e-mail at guskey@uky.edu, on X at @tguskey, or at www.tguskey.com.

CHAPTER 1

....

PARENTS' AND FAMILIES' PERSPECTIVES ON GRADING AND REPORTING REFORMS

In schools throughout the world today, educators are reforming the way they grade and report student learning. The school leaders and teachers in these schools recognize that many of their current grading policies and practices are out-of-date and sorely inadequate. They also realize that these policies and practices don't align well with recent changes in school curriculums, instructional strategies, and procedures for assessing student learning. Yet despite their commitment and good intentions, most of these dedicated educators are struggling in their reform efforts.

What often eludes so many of these hard-working school leaders and teachers is that to reform grading and reporting means challenging some of education's longest held and most firmly entrenched traditions. It means altering policies and practices that have been a part of schooling for generations. Challenging these well-established traditions prompts concern among all stakeholders and serious opposition from some. In many cases, the most adamant opposition to grading and reporting reforms comes from parents and families.

School leaders and teachers are often surprised by this staunch opposition. Parents and families rarely oppose reasonable changes in schooling. They know the education their children need to succeed in the world today must be different from the education they received in schools decades ago. Advances in technology, combined with numerous societal changes, have drastically altered the knowledge and skills children need today to succeed in school and in any career or profession they may choose.

So why are parents and families so opposed to reforms in grading and reporting? What makes grading reform such a lightning rod for controversy and contention? Surveys investigating this issue find that parents' and families' opposition to changes in grading stems from two major concerns (Guskey & Link, 2019; Guskey et al., 2011). First and foremost, they don't see the need for change. Grading reforms involve altering traditions that have remained relatively constant in schools for the past century (see Guskey & Brookhart, 2019). Challenging those traditions means disrupting the security they provide. It means pushing all stakeholders, and especially parents and families, from what is well-known and familiar to something unknown and uncertain, with no guarantee that the new will be better.

Parents and families don't necessarily support current grading policies or the idiosyncratic grading practices of individual teachers, but at least they understand them. These policies and practices are the same as they experienced when they were in school. Changing grading and reporting not only challenges that understanding, it diminishes parents' and families' confidence in their ability to guide their children in successfully negotiating the grading process.

Second, parents and families are keenly aware of the importance attached to grades by educators and others. Grades are the primary criteria used to determine if their child will be promoted from one grade level to the next. Grades affect their child's eligibility for advanced classes and participation in sports and other extracurricular activities. Grades are a major factor in the college admission process and entry into many careers. Changing grading and reporting could significantly impact these crucial decisions that affect their child in school and beyond (see Franklin et al., 2016).

To succeed in grading reforms, school leaders and teachers must be aware of and anticipate these concerns. But even more important, they must know how to address them. Those leading grading reform efforts must be prepared to discuss these concerns openly and honestly. They need to combine that openness with a deep understanding of the change process and the conditions necessary for successful and sustained change. They must know how to frame grading reforms in ways that make sense to parents and families and be ready to describe both the practical advantages and educational value of the changes they advocate. Furthermore, they must be able to engage parents and families as meaningful partners in the change process so that they become allies and supporters of grading reforms rather than challengers and opponents.

Parents and families who trust their children's school leaders and teachers tend to be more engaged with and supportive of educational programs (Santiago et al., 2016). The regularity and transparency of the messages parents and families receive from educators are major contributors to that trust. The quality of that communication, however, seems to matter more than the quantity (Adams & Christenson, 2000). This book is designed to provide school leaders and teachers with the awareness, knowledge, understanding, and skills they need to develop that trust among the parents and families with whom they work.

PURPOSE

This book is about parents' and families' concerns regarding grading reforms and how to address those concerns. It is not designed to be a comprehensive analysis of parents' and families' perspectives on education. Other excellent resources provide school leaders and teachers with that insight, especially *Parents and Teachers: Perspectives, Interactions, and Relationships*, edited by Francesco Arcidiacono (2021); *School, Family, and Community Partnerships: Your Handbook for Action* by Joyce Epstein and Associates (2009); and *Helping Parents Understand Schools: A Different Perspective on Education and Schooling in America* by Lyndon Furst (2017). This book also does not offer detailed descriptions of the essential aspects of grading reform. Books such as *On Your Mark: Challenging the Conventions of Grading and Reporting* (Guskey, 2015) and *Get Set, Go! Creating Successful Grading and Reporting Systems* (Guskey, 2020) are specifically designed to do that.

Instead, this book is intended to be a brief, extremely practical, no-nonsense guide to help school leaders and teachers successfully implement meaningful reforms in grading and reporting student learning. The goal is to help reform leaders recognize the concerns of parents and families regarding grading issues, understand the reasons behind those concerns, and know how to address those concerns in meaningful and effective ways.

The need for this book was prompted by an extensive analysis we conducted of press reports and other accounts of school districts that had attempted grading reforms but failed miserably in their efforts (see Guskey, 2021a, 2021b). Studying these reports helped pinpoint the pitfalls school leaders and teachers need to anticipate and gave insight into how to avoid them.

It also helped identify both failed approaches to grading reform and alternative approaches more likely to succeed, and showed how to weigh various options when the evidence is unclear. Following the advice offered on these pages will not necessarily guarantee success in every grading reform effort. Nevertheless, the existing evidence shows that ignoring these issues will most certainly result in failure.

CHAPTER DESCRIPTIONS

The seven following chapters in this book describe the issues most crucial to gaining parents' and families' support for grading reforms and how to engage them as genuine partners in the reform process.

Chapter 2: Understand the Change Process

School leaders and teachers often fail in their reform efforts because they don't understand the critical aspects and subtle nuances of the change process. In particular, they make the mistake of trying to change parents' and families' attitudes and beliefs directly through persuasive presentations, discussions, and individual conversations. Strong evidence shows, however, that attitudes and beliefs are rarely changed through verbal persuasion. Instead, they are formed and altered primarily through personal experience. This chapter shows how a focus on changing parents', families', and students' experiences with grading and reporting provides the key to reform success.

Chapter 3: Clarify the Purpose of Grading

Before considering the advantages or shortcomings of changes in grading and reporting, parents and families want to understand *why* change is necessary. This requires school leaders and teachers first to clarify the purpose of grading and reporting. Making the purpose clear, transparent, and well understood by all stakeholders provides the basis for examining all grading policies and practices to determine if they align with that specified purpose.

Chapter 4: Distinguish the Three Components of Computerized Grading Programs

Nearly all schools today use computerized grading programs to simplify grading and reporting tasks. Although these programs vary widely in their format and ease of use, all include three basic components: (1) a gradebook, (2) a report card, and (3) a permanent record or transcript. To use and interpret these components correctly, school leaders and teachers must help parents and families understand the function of these components and the purpose each is designed to serve. Vital to that understanding is the recognition that not everything recorded in the gradebook will be used in determining students' report card grades.

Chapter 5: Keep the Report Card Simple and Family Friendly

Many grading reform initiatives fail because educators make the report card far too complicated and difficult for parents and families to interpret. This chapter clarifies what parents and families want in a report card and what they find most useful. It describes how to find the crucial balance between being detailed enough to provide meaningful information on which parents and families can act, but not so detailed that it overwhelms them with information they don't understand and don't know how to use.

Chapter 6: Consider How Parents and Families Interpret Labels

Although choosing the labels used to describe different levels of student performance may seem a simple task, how parents and families interpret those labels is vitally important. Some commonly used labels draw significant criticism from parents and families due to their lack of specificity and their ambiguity. This chapter reviews what is known about parents' and families' reactions to different label terms and outlines procedures for selecting labels that are clear, concise, meaningful, and easy for parents and families to interpret.

Chapter 7: Replace Old Traditions With New Traditions

Many long-established school traditions are based on grades. Examples include the honor roll, the determination of students' class rank, procedures for selecting a class valedictorian, and assigning a single grade to students for each subject area or class. Reforming grading doesn't require completely abandoning these traditions. However, it does require replacing traditions that have long outlived their usefulness with new traditions that are better for students and more educationally sound. This chapter describes some of these long-held traditions, explains why they should be changed, and presents new traditions that can be implemented in their place that benefit students, improve communication between school and home, and will likely be supported by parents and families.

Chapter 8: Focus on a Reporting System

Many school leaders and teachers struggle in grading reform efforts because they focus exclusively on changes in the report card. Successful reform leaders take a more holistic approach and consider an entire *reporting system* that includes the many ways educators can communicate information about students' performance in school to parents and families. These include not only report cards and formal parent–teacher conferences but the wide range of less formal means of communication, such as home visits, phone calls, e-mail, and text messages. This chapter discusses the different components of a comprehensive reporting system and how to take advantage of the positive aspects of each.

CONCLUSION

No simple recipe can assure success in grading and reporting reforms. No specific set of steps or planning procedures can guarantee trouble-free implementation, unfettered by controversy or contention. As we described earlier, changing grading means challenging the longest held and most firmly established traditions that we have in education. In addition, context differences can be very influential. What works in one school, district, or jurisdiction may not work as well in another school community with different students, teachers, school leaders, and parents and families. Adaptations to the unique characteristics of that community are essential.

Nevertheless, the school leaders and teachers most likely to succeed in grading reform efforts are those who understand parents' and families' perspectives on grading and reporting, recognize the issues most important to them, and engage them as true partners in the reform process.

All too often, educators' relations with parents and families are one-sided conversations rather than genuine partnerships (Rebora, 2022). Real partnerships are "concerned with building *reciprocal* relationships, *shared* responsibility, and *joint work* across settings" (Dugan, 2022, p. 20, emphasis added). They focus on mutual understanding, reciprocal respect, and shared concern for doing what is best for students.

To establish such partnerships, reform leaders must anticipate parents' and families' concerns and approach the reform process in ways that meaningfully address those concerns. They need to recognize that parents and families who initially resist grading and reporting reforms are not antagonistic by nature, nor are they collectively opposed to change. Their resistance comes instead from genuine concern for the well-being of students, especially their own children (see Franklin et al., 2016).

Successful school leaders and teachers do not ignore opposition to grading reforms, nor do they try to avoid it. Instead, they anticipate opposition and address it directly with patience, purpose, and resolve. They work to engage parents and families as partners in the reform effort rather than simply impose reforms upon them. By anticipating concerns, addressing those concerns as part of the reform process, and engaging parents and families as true partners throughout, school leaders and teachers can guarantee more trouble-free implementation of grading reform and far greater success.

REFERENCES

Adams, K. S., & Christenson, S. L. (2000). Trust and the family–school relationship examination of parent–teacher differences in elementary and secondary grades. *Journal of School Psychology, 38*(5), 477–497.

Arcidiacono, F. (Ed.). (2021). *Parents and teachers: Perspectives, interactions, and relationships.* Nova Science Publishers.

Dugan, J. (2022). Co-constructing family engagement. *Educational Leadership, 80*(1), 20–26.

Epstein, J., & Associates. (2009). *School, family, and community partnerships: Your handbook for action* (3rd ed.). Corwin Press.

Franklin, A., Buckmiller, T., & Kruse, J. (2016). Vocal and vehement: Understanding parents' aversion to standards-based grading. *International Journal of Social Science Studies, 4*(11), 19–29. https://doi.org/10.11114/ijsss.v4i11.1923

Furst, L. G. (2017). *Helping parents understand schools: A different perspective on education and schooling in America.* Information Age Publishing.

Guskey, T. R. (2015). *On your mark: Challenging the conventions of grading and reporting.* Solution Tree.

Guskey, T. R. (2020). *Get set, go! Creating successful grading and reporting systems.* Solution Tree.

Guskey, T. R. (2021a). Learning from failures: Lessons from unsuccessful grading reform initiatives. *NASSP Bulletin, 105*(3), 192–199.

Guskey, T. R. (2021b). Undoing the traditions of grading and reporting. *The School Administrator, 78*(5), 32–35.

Guskey, T. R., & Brookhart, S. M. (Eds.). (2019). *What we know about grading: What works, what doesn't, and what's next?* ASCD.

Guskey, T. R., & Link, L. J. (2019, April). *Understanding different stakeholders' views on homework and grading* [Paper presentation]. Annual Meeting of the American Educational Research Association, Toronto, ON, Canada.

Guskey, T. R., Swan, G. M., & Jung, L. A. (2011, April). *Parents' and teachers' perceptions of standards-based and traditional report cards* [Paper presentation]. Annual Meeting of the American Educational Research Association, New Orleans, LA.

Rebora, A. (2022). Reader's guide: Family engagement reimagined. *Educational Leadership, 80*(1), 7.

Santiago, R., Garbacz, S., Beattie, R., & Dragoo, C. (2016). Parent-teacher relationships in elementary school: An examination of parent-teacher trust. *Psychology in the Schools, 53*(10), 1003–1017.

CHAPTER 2

....

UNDERSTAND THE CHANGE PROCESS

Successful grading and reporting reform requires a deep understanding of the change process. School leaders and teachers need to know what facilitates change, what restricts change, and what prevents change entirely. They also need to be aware of change strategies that don't work so those can be avoided and to focus on those that do work in order to ensure reform initiatives have the best chance of success.

We begin this chapter with a discussion of popular change strategies that evidence indicates don't work and explain why these strategies so rarely succeed. This will shed new light on why so many well-intentioned grading and reporting reform efforts end in failure. We then consider an alternative approach and new model for change, along with its specific implications for gaining acceptance and support from parents and families. Finally, we turn to applications of this new change model and describe examples of its use in implementing successful grading and reporting reforms across all education levels.

WHAT DOESN'T WORK?

Many school leaders and teachers attempt to change parents' and families' attitudes and beliefs about grading through logical arguments and personal persuasion. They believe that impassioned presentations and discussions that describe grading reform as a "moral imperative" will win the hearts and minds of all stakeholders, especially parents and families. In these presentations, they focus on the anomalies and hidden contradictions in many current grading practices and describe how these need to be "fixed." They may describe, for example, how educators claim that grades accurately reflect student learning but then point out how teachers frequently raise the grades of students who show exceptional effort or lower the grades of students who misbehave in class or fail to turn in assignments on time.

Despite their good intentions, most school leaders and teachers quickly discover that these attempts at logical persuasion rarely produce significant or enduring change in parents' and families' attitudes and beliefs about grading. Regardless of how fervent and impassioned the presentation, the simple truth is that logical arguments rarely change people. As American writer Dale Carnegie (1936) pointed out decades ago, "When dealing with people, remember you are not dealing with creatures of logic, but with creatures of emotion." Similarly, renowned psychologist Edward de Bono noted, "Logic will never change emotion or perception" (quoted in Balakrishnan, 2007).

> *Logical arguments rarely change people.*

People's attitudes and beliefs are not intellectually derived from logic or careful reasoning (Kolbert, 2017). They are derived instead from *personal experience* and *desire*. In other words, they come from what people have known and from what they want. This fundamental principle will be the basis of our discussion in Chapter 3 when we turn to the crucial importance of addressing *why* before *what*.

Unfortunately for school leaders and teachers, most of the articles they read about grading reform, and most of the presentations they hear from consultants advocating reforms in grading, ignore this fundamental principle. In nearly all instances, those articles and presentations focus on *what* should be changed. School leaders and teachers are told they need to revise report cards, change grading scales, and adopt new policies regarding zeros, homework, turning in late assignments, and retaking assessments. Trusting this advice, they move forward with these structural changes, unaware of the many problems that lie ahead because the experiences and desires of parents and families were ignored. When objections are raised and pushback occurs, they are caught ill-informed and unprepared, and their well-intentioned reform initiatives fall apart.

WHAT DOES WORK?

The most important first step in understanding the change process and how to facilitate change is to know what various stakeholders want and why they want it. In other words, what do they desire and how do grading reforms relate to those desires? Retired Harvard Business School professor John Kotter (2012) describes this as "communicating for buy-in." It doesn't mean that stakeholders' desires will dictate precisely what the reforms will be. Instead, it implies that what stakeholders say they want must be acknowledged and well understood and then used to frame the approach to change.

When parents and families are asked what they truly want from schools, school leaders, and teachers, their answers are consistent and self-evident. Across all grade levels, parents and families want the following for their children:

- To be successful in school

- To feel good about being in school and confident in their ability to learn

- To feel valued, cared for, and have a sense of belonging in school

- To have new experiences, see opportunities, and believe the factors that determine their success are within their control (Guskey & Link, 2019; Guskey et al., 2022)

To better ensure their children develop this sense of belonging and success, parents and families want regular and specific feedback from teachers about how their children are doing in school. They want to know when their children are doing well and when they're experiencing any problems or learning difficulties. Most importantly, they want this information in a form they can easily understand and readily use (Guskey, 2002a).

THE PERSPECTIVES OF PARENTS AND FAMILIES MUST BE:

- Recognized and acknowledged

- Deeply understood

- Used to frame reform initiatives

How can reform efforts be organized to take into account what parents and families truly want? How can we approach change in a way that leads to the implementation of more effective grading policies and practices *and* addresses these crucial wants and desires? To do this requires a new approach to reform, a new vision of the change process, and an alternative model of change.

AREAS OF CHANGE

Researchers investigating the change process in education, especially through the professional learning experiences of educators, generally agree that the primary goal of these efforts is to bring about change in three areas. Specifically, they are designed to prompt change in

- teachers' attitudes and beliefs,

- teachers' classroom practices, and

- student learning outcomes (Learning Forward, 2022).

For those leading change efforts, however, the important question is, *In what order do these changes occur?* In other words, what is the typical sequence of these change events? They don't happen simultaneously, and reform leaders and teachers who hope to succeed must consider the order to determine where their attention should be focused and what critical needs must be addressed.

Research shows that the relationship among these three areas of change is detailed and highly complex (Fullan, 2015; Guskey, 2002b). In addition, that relationship is undoubtedly reciprocal to some degree (Guskey, 2020). Nevertheless, to succeed in reform efforts, school leaders and teachers must consider the order of outcomes most likely to result in desired change and the endurance of that change (see Guskey, 2000).

> *To succeed in reform efforts, school leaders and teachers must consider the order of outcomes most likely to result in desired change and the endurance of that change (see Guskey, 2000).*

Over the years, professional learning activities in education have typically set out first to change educators' attitudes, beliefs, perceptions, and dispositions. Efforts might be made, for example, to convince teachers that a new instructional method is more effective, that inclusive classrooms are better for all students, or that a different approach to classroom assessments can improve students' learning. These efforts are based on the assumption that change in educators' attitudes and beliefs will lead to specific changes in school and classroom practices, which, in turn, will result in improvements in student learning outcomes. This perspective on change evolved largely from a model developed by early change theorists such as Kurt Lewin (1935), who derived many of his ideas about affecting change from psychotherapeutic models.

More recent research on educator change, however, indicates that the assumptions of this model are inaccurate, especially with regard to professional learning activities involving experienced educators. Specifically, even the most carefully designed professional learning activities rarely result in significant change in educators' attitudes and beliefs (Guskey & Huberman, 1995; Putnam & Borko, 2000). For that reason, a different model that reexamines the process of change under these special conditions is needed to guide the creation of more effective professional learning experiences for educators.

> *Even the most carefully designed professional learning activities rarely result in significant change in educators' attitudes and beliefs (Guskey & Huberman, 1995; Putnam & Borko, 2000).*

ALTERNATIVE MODEL OF CHANGE

An alternative approach to change in education is illustrated below. According to this alternative model, significant change in educators' attitudes and beliefs takes place only *after* positive change in student learning outcomes are evident. These changes in student learning result, of course, from specific changes educators have made in their classroom or school practices. For example, they might be the result of a new instructional approach, the use of new materials or curriculums, new classroom policies and practices, or simply some modification in the way teachers grade and report student learning progress. Whatever the case, this model indicates that significant change in educators' attitudes and beliefs is contingent upon evidence of change in the learning outcomes of their students.

> *Significant change in educators' attitudes and beliefs takes place only after positive change in student learning outcomes are evident.*

ALTERNATIVE MODEL OF CHANGE

SOURCE: Adapted from Guskey, 2020

The crucial point of this model is that professional learning activities alone seldom yield significant change in educators' attitudes, beliefs, perceptions, or dispositions. Educators are simply not changed by what they are told or by what they are shown. They change based on *what they experience*. It is the experience of successful implementation that prompts change in educators' attitudes, beliefs, perceptions, or dispositions. Educators believe something works when they see that it works. *Experience shapes their attitudes and beliefs.* Thus, according to the model, the key element in significant change in educators' attitudes and beliefs is clear evidence of improvement in the learning outcomes of their students (Guskey, 1986, 2002b, 2020).

For a video explanation of the model, see the YouTube video, "Guskey's Model of Teacher Change":

bit.ly/3KoAYb1

It is important to keep in mind that *learning outcomes* in this model are broadly defined to include not only cognitive and achievement measures but also the wide range of student affective, behavioral, and noncognitive outcomes. They may consist of evidence on students' engagement in class activities; motivation for learning; or attitudes toward school, toward the class, and toward themselves as learners. In other words, learning outcomes include whatever evidence educators use to judge the effectiveness of their teaching, their classroom or school practices, and their success with students.

The premise of this model of change is that change is primarily an experientially based learning process for educators. Practices that are found to work—that is, those found to be useful in motivating students, managing students' learning, or helping students attain desired learning outcomes—are retained and repeated. Those that don't work or that fail to yield any tangible evidence of improvement are generally abandoned. A key factor in the endurance of any change in classroom or school practices and procedures, therefore, is demonstrable results in terms of student outcomes.

According to this model, when educators see that a new program or innovation helps students and enhances learning outcomes, then, and perhaps *only* then, is significant change in their attitudes and beliefs likely to occur.

As is true of any model of complex phenomena, this model of change oversimplifies the change process somewhat, and exceptions certainly exist. For example, educators must believe there is the possibility for improvement before they will consider major revisions in their current practices.

Furthermore, the change process may be more cyclical than linear (Huberman, 1992, 1995). In other words, changes in attitudes and beliefs are likely to spur additional changes in practice that bring further change in student learning, and so on (Huberman, 1983, 1985). Still, the consistency of the results from diverse studies of teacher change provides strong support for this model (for resources, see Guskey, 1986, 1989, 2002b, 2020).

> *Changes in attitudes and beliefs are likely to spur additional changes in practice that bring further change in student learning, and so on (Huberman, 1983, 1985).*

IMPLICATIONS OF THE MODEL

The basic proposition of this alternative model of change—that *experience shapes attitudes and beliefs*—yields two powerful implications for school leaders and teachers engaged in grading reforms. These implications are essential in planning and implementing successful reform initiatives and in gaining the support of parents and families.

Don't Try to Change Attitudes and Beliefs Directly

As we've emphasized throughout this chapter, those who set out to change stakeholders' attitudes and beliefs directly are likely doomed to failure. Sure, some modest change may be possible and definitely should be sought. We would certainly hope, for example, that when parents and families are presented with new ideas and supporting evidence about the need to reform grading and reporting, their attitudes will at least be moved from cynical to skeptical. While they may not be fully persuaded or convinced, they may agree to engage in further discussions and consider new points of view. Keep in mind, however, that commitment to a new approach, confidence that it will work, and trust that it will be better almost never occur prior to implementation. The best that can be hoped for is a tentative, "I'm not sure, but let's give it a try." If by giving it a try parents and families see benefits for their children and personal evidence of improvement in the grading and reporting process, then, and perhaps only then, will significant change in their attitudes and beliefs occur.

> *Commitment to a new approach, confidence that it will work, and trust that it will be better almost never occur prior to implementation.*

A classic example of this change process is depicted in the 2000 film *Remember the Titans*, starring Denzel Washington. Based on a true story, the film portrays African-American coach Herman Boone's efforts to integrate a high school football team in Alexandria, Virginia, in the early 1970s. Due to the changes in the personal experiences of these young athletes, their attitudes and beliefs about respect, trust, honor, and race are completely transformed. The message is this: If you can find ways to meaningfully change individuals' personal experiences, significant change in their attitudes and beliefs will follow.

Don't Expect Changes in Grading and Reporting to Improve Student Achievement

School leaders and teachers often are asked what results they expect from grading reforms. One of the most frequent questions is whether changes in grading and reporting will improve student achievement. Most school leaders and teachers have probably read blogs or heard consultants tell anecdotes about remarkable turnarounds in schools that have reformed their grading practices. But in truth, few well-designed, systematic studies have linked the implementation of grading reforms to specific improvements in student achievement (see Brookhart et al., 2016; Guskey & Brookhart, 2019; Link & Guskey, 2022). This is true even of reforms associated with standards-based or competency-based grading (for noted exceptions, see Pollio & Hochbein, 2015, and the review of research by Welsh, 2019).

But in a larger sense, why would we expect grading reforms to affect student achievement? Changing grading doesn't alter the curriculum (i.e., what is taught) or instruction (i.e., how it is taught)—the two major factors that determine what and how well students learn. Any potential impact of grading reform on curriculum or instruction would be tangential at best (Guskey & Jung, 2013).

> *Grading and reporting reforms are about communicating more accurate and more meaningful information to parents, families, and students* in order to provide the basis for improving student learning.

Grading and reporting reforms are about communicating more accurate and more meaningful information to parents, families, and students *in order to provide the basis for improving student learning*. Whether or not this *leads* to specific improvements in student achievement depends not only on the quality of that information but how that information is used (Guskey, 2008). Nevertheless, establishing that basis is a powerful first step forward in making those improvements.

USING THE MODEL TO FACILITATE CHANGE

The alternative model of change presented above provided the basis for gaining the support of parents and families for a large-scale grading and reporting reform initiative in Kentucky. We described this program in an article published in *Kappan* (Guskey et al., 2011) and in an *Education Week* blog (see Guskey, 2016).

Our primary goal in designing this program was to encourage students to focus more on learning and less on what it takes to get a high grade. We also wanted parents and families to see grades as a means of communication between teachers and homes rather than as the currency students need to advance in school. Equally important, we wanted parents and families to understand that abandoning certain traditional grading practices would enhance efforts to help all students learn better and improve their performance in school.

In the initial stages of implementation, we made no attempt to change parents' and families' attitudes and beliefs about grading through logical arguments or emotional appeals. We simply notified parents and families through e-mail messages and letters about the changes in grading and reporting we planned and then explained the rationale behind those changes. Specifically, we indicated that on the report card, (1) achievement and nonachievement factors of school performance would be reported separately, (2) instead of percentage grades, a five-level, *A-F* grading scale would be used, similar to colleges and university grading systems, and (3) subject area and course grades would be broken down to show students' performance in academic strands or subcategories. Our hope was to change parents' and families' experience with grading and report cards, which we believed would then lead to their support.

In the first two grading periods of the initial year of implementation, we introduced parents and families to these changes in grading and reporting by providing them with two different report cards either online or as paper copies sent home. The first was the older, traditional report card that listed a single grade for each subject area or course. This report card is typical of those produced by online grading programs and looks much like the report card parents received when they were in school.

The second was our new, standards-based report card. It included photographs of the teachers of each subject area or course—an idea we saw used in report cards from several Canadian school districts. In addition to an achievement grade, it reported separate marks for student behaviors related to homework completion, cooperation, respect, punctuality in turning in assignments, and class participation. Besides the overall subject area or course achievement grade, it included a breakdown of students' performance in subcategories of the subject area or course. For example, students' performance in language arts was broken down into the subcategories of reading, writing, listening, speaking, and language skills.

After they had received both report cards for two quarterly grading periods and compared them side by side, we surveyed parents and families to ask which report card they preferred. Invariably, nearly all chose the new, standards-based report card. Why? Because it's simply better. It gives parents and families the detailed information they need to track their child's performance in school. It offers students valuable feedback regarding their progress on explicit learning goals. In addition, it provides guidance and direction to parents, families, and students in improvement efforts. As a result, parents and families became our strongest advocates for change. Experiencing the new form and seeing the improvements it brought influenced their attitudes and beliefs about grading reform.

This alternative model of change appears to hold true for teachers as well. Few teachers leave seminars, workshops, or professional learning sessions convinced that change in grading and reporting will bring improvements or make much difference. It would be an exaggeration to say they are committed to the process or confident that the new grading polices and practice will work. At best, some may be cautiously optimistic. The majority are probably skeptical but at least willing to give it a try.

But when they try and see evidence that it works, their attitudes and beliefs start to change. They hear students talking about what they need to learn better rather than how they can earn more points. They see students helping each other because the learning goals are clear for everyone. They get fewer questions from parents and families about how a grade was determined and more about how they can help with improvements. Although most teachers report that the change initially requires extra work, they believe it's worthwhile because of the differences they see in students and their parents and families.

> *Successful reform leaders focus first on changing the experiences of parents, families, students, and teachers with grading.*

Successful reform leaders focus first on changing the experiences of parents, families, students, and teachers with grading. They find ways to provide meaningful evidence on the advantages of new grading and reporting procedures to these different stakeholders so they see how the reforms benefit them. When they personally experience the benefits, change in their attitudes will almost certainly follow.

- In what ways is this approach to change responsive to what parents desire for their children?

- How might it be applied (or adapted) for your particular context?

SUMMARY

To succeed in implementing grading reforms and in gaining the support of parents and families requires a thorough understanding of the change process. School leaders and teachers must know what actions facilitate change and which are likely to be impediments. In particular, they must understand the order of change events so they know how best to invest their time and energy.

Efforts to directly change parents' and families' attitudes and beliefs about grading rarely succeed. Any changes that are achieved tend to be modest, fleeting, and seldom sustained when difficulties are encountered or objections raised.

The alternative model of change presented in this chapter is derived from the premise that attitudes and beliefs are shaped by peoples' experience and desires. Efforts to change parents' and families' attitudes and beliefs must therefore focus on changing their experiences with grading, while acknowledging and directly addressing what they want and believe they need.

The alternative model of change offers an extremely optimistic perspective on the potential of grading reform efforts. It shows that while the change process is complex, it is not haphazard. Thoughtfully attending to the order of change events described in the model not only facilitates change, it also contributes to the endurance and longevity of change. As a result, even reform efforts that challenge some of education's longest-held traditions are likely to be far more powerful, much more effective, and longer sustained.

To successfully implement reforms in grading and reporting, school leaders and teachers must engage parents and families as partners in the change process. Educators must focus on *working with* parents and families rather than *working on* them.

> *Educators must focus on working with parents and families rather than working on them.*

They must help parents and families experience the positive results that change can bring, and they must ensure those positive results come early in the implementation process. The support of parents and families comes from seeing rather quickly that the grading reforms make a difference in outcomes they consider important.

REFERENCES

Balakrishnan, A. (2007, April 23). Edward de Bono: "Iraq? They just need to think it through." *The Guardian.* https://www.theguardian.com/education/2007/apr/24/highereducation-profile.academicexperts

Brookhart, S. M., Guskey, T. R., Bowers, A. J., McMillan, J. H., Smith, J. K., Smith, L. F., Stevens, M. T., & Welsh, M. J. (2016). A century of grading research: Meaning and value in the most common educational measure. *Review of Educational Research, 86*(4), 803–848.

Carnegie, D. (1936). *How to win friends and influence people.* Gallery Books.

Fullan, M. G. (2015). *The new meaning of educational change* (5th ed.). Teachers College Press.

Guskey, T. R. (1986). Staff development and the process of teacher change. *Educational Researcher, 15*(5), 5–12.

Guskey, T. R. (1989). Attitude and perceptual change in teachers. *International Journal of Educational Research, 13*(4), 439–453.

Guskey, T. R. (2000). *Evaluating professional development.* Corwin Press.

Guskey, T. R. (2002a). *How's my kid doing? A parents' guide to grades, marks, and report cards.* Jossey Bass.

Guskey, T. R. (2002b). Professional development and teacher change. *Teachers and Teaching: Theory and Practice, 8*(3/4), 381–391.

Guskey, T. R. (2008). The rest of the story. *Educational Leadership, 65*(4), 28–35.

Guskey, T. R. (2016, April 9). *Experience shapes attitudes and beliefs.* Education Week Blog. http://mobile.edweek.org/c.jsp?cid=25920011&item=http%3A%2F%2Fapi.edweek.org%2Fv1%2Fblog%2F100%2F%3Fuuid%3D57727

Guskey, T. R. (2020). Flip the script on change: Experience shapes teachers' attitudes and beliefs. *The Learning Professional, 41*(2), 18–22.

Guskey, T. R., & Brookhart, S. M. (Eds.). (2019). *What we know about grading: What works, what doesn't, and what's next?* ASCD.

Guskey, T. R., & Huberman, M. (Eds.). (1995). *Professional development in education: New paradigms and practices.* Teachers College Press.

Guskey, T. R., & Jung, L. A. (2013). *Answers to essential questions about standards, assessments, grading, and reporting.* Corwin Press.

Guskey, T. R., & Link, L. J. (2019, April). *Understanding different stakeholders' views on homework and grading* [Paper presentation]. Annual Meeting of the American Educational Research Association, Toronto, ON, Canada.

Guskey, T. R., Link, L. J., & Link, N. G. (2022, April). *Understanding our differences: Analyzing stakeholders' views on homework, assessment, and grading* [Paper presentation]. Annual Meeting of the American Educational Research Association, San Diego, CA.

Guskey, T. R., Swan, G. M., & Jung, L. A. (2011). Grades that mean something: Kentucky develops standards-based report cards. *Phi Delta Kappan, 93*(2), 52–57.

Huberman, M. (1983). Recipes for busy teachers. *Knowledge: Creation, Diffusion, Utilization, 4*, 478–510.

Huberman, M. (1985). What knowledge is of most worth to teachers? A knowledge-use perspective. *Teaching and Teacher Education, 1*, 251–262.

Huberman, M. (1992). Teacher development and instructional mastery. In A. Hargreaves & M. G. Fullan (Eds.), *Understand teacher development* (pp. 122–142). Teachers College Press.

Huberman, M. (1995). Professional careers and professional development: Some intersections. In T. R. Guskey & M. Huberman (Eds.), *Professional development in education: New paradigms and practices* (pp. 193–224). Teachers College Press.

Kolbert, E. (2017, February 27). Why facts don't change our minds: New discoveries about the human mind show the limitations of reason. *The New Yorker.* https://www.new yorker.com/magazine/2017/02/27/why-facts-dont-change-our-minds

Kotter, J. P. (2012). *Leading change.* Harvard Business Review Press.

Learning Forward. (2022). *Standards for professional learning.* Author. https://standards .learningforward.org/standards-for-professional-learning/

Lewin, K. (1935). *A dynamic theory of personality.* McGraw Hill.

Link, L. J., & Guskey, T. R. (2022). Is standards-based grading effective? *Theory Into Practice, 61*(4), 406–417.

Pollio, M., & Hochbein, C. (2015). The association between standards-based grading and standardized test scores in a high school reform model. *Teachers College Record, 117*(11), 1–28.

Putnam, R. T., & Borko, H. (2000). What do new views of knowledge and thinking have to say about research on teacher learning? *Educational Researcher, 29*(1), 4–15.

Welsh, M. (2019). Standards-based grading. In T. R. Guskey & S. M. Brookhart (Eds.), *What we know about grading: What works, what doesn't, and what's next* (pp. 133–144). ASCD.

CHAPTER 3

····························

CLARIFY THE PURPOSE OF GRADING

When asked about fairness in grading, the most frequent complaint of parents, families, and students is the lack of consistency in policies and practices among teachers *in the same school* (Guskey & Link, 2019; Guskey et al., 2022). Each time students change classes, the rules for grading change. What counts as part of the grade, what doesn't count, and how different aspects of performance are weighted in determining the grade—all can be different.

This lack of consistency leads many students to see grading as a game they must learn to play in order to succeed in school, and some students play the game quite well. They become strategists in the grading game, constantly tallying points and calculating the minimum scores they must attain to get the grade they want. But for other students, the grading game remains a mysterious puzzle they must try to decipher in every class, and many struggle in that effort. They might recognize that they're not doing well but don't find the guidance they receive from teachers to "pay attention" and "try harder" to be particularly helpful. So, when a parent asks at the dinner table, "What grade are you going to get in this class?" the student responds in all honesty, "I don't know."

A major reason for this inconsistency in teachers' grading policies and practices is lack of agreement on the purpose of grading. Teachers frequently don't agree on why they are giving grades in the first place. When neither teachers nor school leaders agree on

> *Teachers frequently don't agree on why they are giving grades in the first place.*

what grades mean or what primary purpose they serve, the procedures used to determine grades and what they represent tend to vary from teacher to teacher, from class to class, and from school to school. That's why the first step in any successful grading reform effort is reaching consensus on the primary purpose of grades and report cards.

THE PURPOSE OF GRADES AND REPORT CARDS

In essence, grades are simply the symbols educators assign to individual pieces of student work or to composite measures of student performance created for report cards and other summary documents (Guskey & Brookhart, 2019). Grades can be letters, numbers, words, symbols, or any set of descriptors that designate different levels of performance. Grades in various forms are used today at every level of education, from preschool and kindergarten through graduate and professional schools, in every country throughout the world.

EXAMPLES OF DIFFERENT FORMS OF GRADES

LETTERS	NUMERALS	DESCRIPTORS	EMOJIS
A	4	Exemplary	😎
B	3	Proficient	🙂
C	2	Developing	😕
D	1	Struggling	😩
F	0	No Evidence	🙁

(From Smith et al., 2023, p. 56)

Successful grading reforms *always* begin with focused discussions on the purpose of grades and the use of report cards (Brookhart, 2011; Guskey & Bailey, 2010). This requires addressing two simple but vitally important questions:

1. *Why* do we assign grades or marks to students' work?

2. *Why* do we summarize and record those summaries on report cards?

These *why* questions *must* be addressed and some consensus *must* be reached before considering *what* issues related to the grading policies and practices need to be changed to align with that purpose.

When researchers ask educators why they assign grades and what purpose the grades serve, the answers of both school leaders and teachers generally fall into one of six broad categories (see Frisbie & Waltman, 1992; Guskey & Bailey, 2001; Linn, 1983; Russell & Airasian, 2011). These purposes include:

1. *To communicate information to families and others.* Grading and reporting provide parents, families, and other interested persons (e.g., guardians, relatives, tutors, coaches, school leaders, etc.) with information about students' achievement, learning progress, and behavior in school. In some instances, grading and reporting also serve to involve parents and families in educational processes.

2. *To provide information to students for self-evaluation.* Grading and reporting offer information to students about their level of achievement and the adequacy of their performance in school. As an important source of feedback, grades and report cards also can help direct students' effort and guide improvements in their academic performance (Guskey, 2022).

3. *To select or group students for specific educational paths or programs.* Grades are the major source of evidence used in making decisions about students' promotion from one grade level to the next. Entry into gifted education programs and honors or advanced classes typically requires high grades. Low grades are often the first indicator of learning problems that may qualify students for special needs services. In addition, grade summaries on transcripts are a major factor considered in the admission process to selective colleges and universities.

4. *To provide incentives for students to learn.* Although some educators debate the issue, extensive evidence shows that grades and other reporting devices influence the effort students put forth and how seriously they regard learning tasks or assessments (Brookhart, 1993; Cameron & Pierce, 1994, 1996; Chastain, 1990).

5. *To evaluate the effectiveness of instructional programs.* Comparisons of grades and other records of students' performance are major sources of evidence used in judging the value and effectiveness of new programs, curriculums, and instructional strategies.

6. *To verify appropriate effort or responsibility on the part of students.* Grades and other reporting devices are also used to document students' effort in learning tasks or responsibility displayed in learning activities. Teachers may raise the grades of students who try hard and behave well in class or lower the grades of students who don't complete homework or fail to turn in assignments on time.

Educators generally agree that all these purposes could be considered valid. They seldom agree, however, on which purpose is most important. If asked to rank order these purposes in terms of their importance, school leaders and teachers typically offer widely varied responses—even those who are staff members from the same school (Link, 2018).

Major Purposes of Grading and Reporting

- To communicate information about students' learning to families and others
- To provide information to students for self-evaluation
- To select or group students for specific educational paths or programs
- To provide incentives for students to learn
- To evaluate the effectiveness of instructional programs
- To verify appropriate effort or responsibility on the part of students

No single reporting device can serve all these purposes well.

When educators don't agree on the primary purpose of grades, they often try to address *all* these purposes with a single reporting device, usually a report card, and end up achieving none very well (Austin & McCann, 1992). No single reporting device can serve *all* these purposes well. In fact, careful inspection shows that some of these purposes are counter to others.

PURPOSES VARY IN APPROPRIATENESS

Suppose, for example, that the educators in a particular school or school district make their primary instructional goal to have *all* their students learn well. As they succeed in achieving their goal, increasing numbers of students demonstrate high levels of achievement and earn the same high grades. As a result, the variation in students' grades diminishes.

This positive outcome fits well if their purpose in grading is to communicate information about students' learning to parents, families, and others or to provide students with self-evaluation information. However, if the purpose of grading is to select students for different educational paths or to evaluate the effectiveness of instructional programs, these same positive results become problematic. Selection and evaluation demand variation in grades. They require grades be widely dispersed in order to differentiate among students and programs. How else can appropriate selections be made or one program judged better than another? Variation in grades is essential to both selection and evaluation. Thus, while one purpose is served well, another purpose is not.

Determining the purpose of grades is the essential starting point in any grading reform effort. All grading actions, procedures, policies, and practices must then be aligned with the agreed-upon purpose.

> **Determining the purpose of grades is the essential starting point in any grading reform effort.**

PARENTS' AND FAMILIES' PERSPECTIVES ON PURPOSE

School leaders who succeed in grading reforms also consider the perspectives of parents and families in determining the purpose of grades and especially the report card. After all, parents and families are the primary recipients of the information included in the report card, especially in the elementary grades.

When asked about the purpose of grades and report cards, parents' and families' generally respond much more consistently than do school leaders and teachers. Overwhelmingly, parents and families indicate that communicating with them is the most important purpose. They regard report cards as one of the most crucial sources of information they receive from teachers about how their children are doing in school, both academically and behaviorally (Guskey et al., 2022).

> **Parents and families indicate that communicating with them is the most important purpose.**

This disparity between the perspectives of educators and those of parents and families is frequently ignored in reform efforts. Because effective grading and reporting is primarily a challenge in effective communication (see Guskey, 1996), these disparities need to be recognized and meaningfully addressed. School leaders must work to lessen these differences and help teachers, parents, and families to reach a common understanding of the purpose of grading before turning to the form or structure of the report card. A clear and concise purpose statement makes all other decisions about grading policies and practices much easier.

STOP AND REFLECT

- Based on your professional experience and what you have just read, draft a sentence or two on the purpose of grading.

- If you are also a parent or guardian, how might this statement of purpose differ from what you just wrote from an educator's perspective (or would it)?

DISAGREE AND COMMIT

A strategy many successful school leaders use to reach consensus on a purpose statement for grading is called *disagree and commit*. Credit for developing this strategy is usually given to Scott McNealy of Sun Microsystems, but it's also attributed to Andrew Grove of Intel and Jeff Bezos of Amazon (Origbo, 2017). The origins of disagree and commit, however, can be traced to the strategies used by military leaders to plan battle campaigns.

Disagree and commit is a decision-making strategy in which individuals are encouraged to disagree while a decision is being made, but once the decision *is* made, *everybody* must commit to it. The approach makes clear *when* conflict and disagreement can be valuable, and when it is disruptive and detrimental. Specifically, disagreement is useful in the early stages of decision-making but harmful after the decision has been made. Disagree and commit is also seen as a way to avoid the consensus trap, in which the lack of consensus results in inaction.

The disagree and commit strategy serves two important purposes:

1. *It communicates that all perspectives have value.* Everyone involved in the decision-making process has the chance to voice their point of view and have it considered.

2. *It helps foster a sense of belonging among individuals in the organization who come to see the essential nature of working together.* With a sense of belonging comes loyalty and a willingness to take the risks involved in innovation (Rowland & Pivcevic, 2022).

Successful leaders often initiate grading reform efforts by leading teachers and staff members through the disagree and commit process. Staff members may include counselors, librarians, technology assistants, instructional coaches, teacher aides, and other school personnel. Many leaders begin by simply asking everyone to write a single sentence describing the purpose of grading or the report card. After briefly discussing these purpose statements, leaders present the six purposes we described earlier and ask everyone to rank those purposes in order of their perceived importance. A brief poll is then taken, tallying which purpose individuals ranked as the most and the least important. Much to the surprise of most participants, this typically reveals striking differences among teachers and staff members.

In the discussion that follows, leaders ask participants to explain why they chose the option they did and why they did not choose another. Clarifying these differences and exploring disagreements provides a framework for moving ahead in developing a purpose statement to which *all* can commit. Keeping in mind that parents and families consistently regard the report card as a primary source of information from teachers about how their children are doing in school adds further credibility to the process.

KEY QUESTIONS IN DEVELOPING A PURPOSE STATEMENT

Three key questions need to be addressed in developing a purpose statement for grading and reporting (Guskey & Bailey, 2010):

1. What information will be communicated?
2. Who is the primary audience for that information?
3. What is the intended goal?

The answers to these three questions provide a framework for determining the optimal form and structure for the report card.

What Information Will Be Communicated?

The best report cards communicate three important kinds of information:

1. What students were expected to learn and be able to do
2. How well they achieved those things

3. Whether or not that level of performance is in line with the learning goals and expectations set for the grade or course at this time in the school year

To make this information meaningful, however, requires a critical balance. Specifically, the information must be precise enough to communicate how well students have learned but not so detailed that it overwhelms parents and families with information they don't understand and don't know how to use.

In Chapter 4 we will discuss how the use of computerized grading programs in most schools allows parents and families to have access to teachers' gradebooks in conjunction with the report card. The detailed information on student performance included in the gradebook helps clarify the summaries provided on the report card and need not be duplicated.

Who Is the Primary Audience for That Information?

Although the audience for other types of reporting tools varies, the primary audience for a report card is almost always parents and families. In upper grades, students are often considered an important audience as well.

Elementary teachers usually communicate with students regularly about their learning progress and where additional work or study may be needed. Elementary report cards serve mostly to bring parents and families up to date on students' learning progress by summarizing the information teachers have recorded in the gradebook.

> *Although the audience for other types of reporting tools varies, the primary audience for a report card is almost always parents and families.*

Middle and high school teachers typically see more students each day and for less time than do their elementary colleagues. As a result, they are usually unable to offer students the same level of individual feedback. Most secondary teachers also believe that older students should take increased responsibility for their own achievement and accomplishments in school (see Guskey & Anderman, 2008). Due to these differences, middle and high school level report cards generally serve to inform parents, families, *and* students about how well students are meeting established learning goals and expectations.

What Is the Intended Goal?

The purpose statement should also indicate how the information included in the report card should be used. This will vary, of course, depending on the primary audience. For parents, families, and others, the report card communicates information about students' academic strengths and difficulties. For students, it recognizes successes and identifies areas where additional study is needed. Most important, however, the report card should be seen as part of a continuous and ongoing reporting process that provides feedback to facilitate improvements in student learning rather than as a culminating, summative evaluation.

> *The report card should be seen as part of a continuous and ongoing reporting process that provides feedback to facilitate improvements in student learning rather than as a culminating, summative evaluation*

QUESTIONS TO ADDRESS IN A PURPOSE STATEMENT FOR GRADING

- What information will be communicated?
- Who is the primary audience for the information?
- What is the intended goal?

STATING THE PURPOSE

To ensure a shared understanding by all stakeholders, the purpose statement should be printed on the report card and included in the introduction of all grading policy documents (Guskey & Bailey, 2010). Adding the purpose statement to the report card makes clear its intent, what information it includes, and how that information should be interpreted. It also helps avoid misinterpretation.

> *Adding the purpose statement to the report card makes clear its intent, what information it includes, and how that information should be interpreted.*

Numerous examples of purpose statements for grading and report cards can be found in *Developing Standards-Based Report Cards* (Guskey & Bailey, 2010). Although these vary widely, all include the three common elements we described. The following is an example from the elementary level:

> *The purpose of this report card is to describe students' learning progress to parents and families, based on our school's learning*

goals for each grade level. It is intended to inform parents and families about learning successes and to guide improvements when needed.

This statement specifies the aim of the report card, for whom the information is intended, and how that information is to be used. It's brief but clear and to the point. An example for the middle school or high school level would be:

The purpose of this report card is to communicate with parents, families, and students about the achievement of specific learning goals. It identifies students' current levels of performance with regard to those goals, areas of strength, and areas where additional time and effort are needed.

This statement identifies parents, families, *and* students as important recipients of the report card's information. It also specifies the information describes students' "current level of performance"—not where they started or an average of scores over the grading period. In addition, it indicates how the information ought to be used.

A third example comes from the American School of Paris, an international school that has been especially thoughtful in their approach to grading and reporting reform:

The primary purpose of grading is to effectively communicate student achievement toward specific standards, at this point in time. A grade should reflect what a student knows and is able to do. Students will receive separate feedback and evaluation on their learning habits, which will not be included in the academic achievement grades.

Two parts of this purpose statement deserve special attention. First is the phrase "at this point in time." By including this phrase, the teachers make clear that they no longer average evidence on students' performance over time to determine grades. Instead, they want grades to represent students' *current* level of achievement and performance; that is, what students now know and can do. In other words, grades are not based on past evidence of where students were but on the most recent evidence of where they are now.

Second, by indicating that "students will receive separate feedback and evaluation on their learning habits," the teachers are emphasizing that achievement grades represent students' performance on specific academic learning goals. Other aspect of students' behavior related to learning habits, such as homework completion, class participation, and punctuality in turning in assignments, will be reported separately. In Chapter 4 we will discuss the process of using multiple grades to report achievement and learning habits separately in greater detail.

The purpose statement that works best will vary depending on the context. Differences across education levels are especially common. For example, the purpose of an elementary report card may differ somewhat from that of a middle school or high school report card. Nevertheless, at all levels it's essential that the purpose be clear to everyone involved in the grading and reporting process— teachers, parents and families, students, and administrators. In that way, everyone understands the report card's intent and can use it appropriately.

> *The purpose statement that works best will vary depending on the context.*

BENEFITS OF A CLEAR PURPOSE STATEMENT

Clarifying the purpose of grading brings several important benefits. A well-designed study by Jessica Gogerty (2016) showed that when the purpose of grading is clearly articulated, teachers become more deliberate in their approach to student learning. They prioritize curriculum standards and adjust their instructional procedures to more closely align the content, format, and difficulty of classroom assessments. Teachers also expressed less tolerance of colleagues who failed to align their teaching and learning practices to the grading purpose. They saw this failure as "negligence" that causes unnecessary confusion for students and families (p. 154). When the grading purpose is made clear, more coordinated efforts to uphold that purpose are expected.

> *When the grading purpose is made clear, more coordinated efforts to uphold that purpose are expected.*

CLARIFYING THE MEANING OF GRADES

Along with specifying the purpose of grading, many school leaders and teachers take the additional step of clarifying the meaning of grades for parents and families. As we described earlier, they stress that grades are simply labels that designate different levels of student performance. These labels may be letters, numbers, words, or symbols. They identify how well students performed learning tasks or achieved specific learning goals. As such, grades serve important formative purposes by helping students, as well as parents and families, know students' current level of achievement. When paired with individualized guidance and direction for improvement, they help direct students' learning progress (Guskey, 2022).

To serve this important formative purpose, however, two essential aspects of grading must be made clear:

1. *Students, parents, and families must understand that grades do not reflect* who *you are as a learner, but* where *you are in your learning journey—and where is* always *temporary.* Knowing where you are is essential to improvement. Informed judgments from teachers about the quality of student performance help students become more thoughtful judges of their own work. They can also help parents and families guide and support students in making improvements. Although a letter, number, word, or symbol offers only a shorthand description of where students are, and additional information is essential to direct progress, grades can provide an important foundation for making improvements.

2. *Grades must never be used to sort, select, or rank students.* Instead of representing how well students have learned, grades are sometimes based on a student's relative standing among classmates. Researchers refer to this as "norm-based grading." When used for these sorting and ranking purposes, students see grades as scarce rewards offered to a select few rather than as recognition of learning success attainable by all. Doing well does not mean learning excellently; it means outdoing your classmates. Helping others is discouraged because for one student to move up in rank, another student must move down.

STOP AND REFLECT

- What are the implications of such "zero sum" grading on the purpose of education? How might it affect the way teachers teach and their goals as teachers?

- How might norm-based grading affect students' values and perceptions of fairness, both in school and beyond? How might it influence their views of themselves as learners?

When grades are based on learning criteria, the performance of classmates is irrelevant. Helping a classmate succeed can actually improve your learning. In this way, criterion-based grading enhances student collaboration by helping students see that everyone—teachers, students, parents, and families—are in this together and seeking to help all students learn well and gain the many positive benefits of learning success.

> *Criterion-based grading enhances student collaboration by helping students see that everyone–teachers, students, parents, and families–are in this together*

HONESTY THROUGH PURPOSE

Students need honest information from their teachers about the quality and adequacy of their performance in school. Parents and families need to know how well their children are doing and whether or not grade-level or course expectations are being met. Although grades should never be the only information about learning that students, parents, and families receive, they can be a meaningful part of that information. When combined with guidance to students, parents, and families on how improvements can be made, grades can become a valuable tool in facilitating students' learning success.

SUMMARY

Reform initiatives that set out to improve grading and reporting procedures *must* begin with inclusive, broad-based discussions involving all stakeholders on the purpose of grading and reporting. These discussions should focus on what information is to be communicated, who is the primary audience or audiences for that information, and what is the intended goal of the communication. Once decisions about purpose are made, other crucial issues involving appropriate grading and reporting policies and practices are much easier to address and more quickly resolved.

REFERENCES

Austin, S., & McCann, R. (1992). *"Here's another arbitrary grade for your collection": A statewide study of grading policies* [Paper presentation]. Annual Meeting of the American Educational Research Association, San Francisco, CA.

Brookhart, S. M. (1993). Teachers' grading practices: Meaning and values. *Journal of Educational Measurement*, 30(2), 123–142.

Brookhart, S. M. (2011). Starting the conversation about grading. *Educational Leadership*, 69(3), 10–14.

Cameron, J., & Pierce, W. D. (1994). Reinforcement, reward, and intrinsic motivation: A meta-analysis. *Review of Educational Research*, 64(3), 363–423.

Cameron, J., & Pierce, W. D. (1996). The debate about rewards and intrinsic motivation: Protests and accusations do not alter the results. *Review of Educational Research*, 66(1), 39–51.

Chastain, K. (1990). Characteristics of graded and ungraded compositions. *Modern Language Journal, 74*(1), 10–14.

Frisbie, D. A., & Waltman, K. K. (1992). Developing a personal grading plan. *Educational Measurement: Issues and Practices, 11*(3), 35–42.

Gogerty, J. (2016). *The influence of district support during implementation of high school standards-based grading practices* [Unpublished doctoral dissertation]. Drake University, Des Moines, Iowa. https://escholarshare.drake.edu/bitstream/handle/2092/2167/Gogerty_drake_0387E_10057.pdf?sequence=1&isAllowed=y

Guskey, T. R. (1996). Reporting on student learning: Lessons from the past—Prescriptions for the future. In T. R. Guskey (Ed.), *Communicating student learning. 1996 yearbook of the association for supervision and curriculum development* (pp. 13–24). ASCD.

Guskey, T. R. (2022). Can grades be an effective form of feedback? *Phi Delta Kappan, 104*(3), 36–41.

Guskey, T. R., & Anderman, E. M. (2008). Students at bat. *Educational Leadership, 66*(3), 8–14.

Guskey, T. R., & Anderman, E. M. (2013). In search of a useful definition of mastery. *Educational Leadership, 71*(4), 18–23.

Guskey, T. R., & Bailey, J. M. (2001). *Developing grading and reporting systems for student learning.* Corwin Press.

Guskey, T. R., & Bailey, J. M. (2010). *Developing standards-based report cards.* Corwin Press.

Guskey, T. R., & Brookhart, S. M. (Eds.). (2019). *What we know about grading: What works, what doesn't, and what's next?* ASCD.

Guskey, T. R., & Link, L. J. (2019, April). *Understanding different stakeholders' views on homework and grading* [Paper presentation]. Annual Meeting of the American Educational Research Association, Toronto, ON, Canada.

Guskey, T. R., Link, L. J., & Link, N. G. (2022, April). *Understanding our differences: Analyzing stakeholders' views on homework, assessment, and grading* [Paper presentation]. Annual Meeting of the American Educational Research Association, San Diego, CA.

Link, L. J. (2018). Teachers' perceptions of grading practices: How pre-service training makes a difference. *Journal of Research in Education, 28*(1), 62–91.

Linn, R. L. (1983). Testing and instruction: Links and distinctions. *Journal of Educational Measurement, 20*(2), 179–189.

Origbo, E. (2017, May 29). *Make "disagree and commit" work for you.* Seeking Mastery. WordPress.com. https://seekingmastery.wordpress.com/2017/05/29/make-disagree-and-commit-work-for-you/

Rowland, D., & Pivcevic. P. (2022, April 8). *Leading change post-pandemic: Belonging. London School of Economics.* LSE Business Review. https://blogs.lse.ac.uk/business review/2022/04/08/leading-change-post-pandemic/

Russell, M. K., & Airasian, P. W. (2011). *Classroom assessment: Concepts and applications* (7th ed.). McGraw-Hill.

Smith, J. K., Lipnevich, A. A., & Guskey, T. R. (2023). *Instructional feedback: The power, the promise, the practice.* Corwin Press.

CHAPTER 4

....

DISTINGUISH THE THREE COMPONENTS OF COMPUTERIZED GRADING PROGRAMS

Ask any teacher today about the report card grade assigned to a particular student and the first thing most will do is open a computerized grading program. They will show you a spreadsheet of the vast array of data they recorded on the student's learning progress and describe how they weighed the different types of information. They will explain how they combined these measures at the end of the grading period and, with the help of the computer, calculated a summary score to the one-hundred-thousandth of a decimal point. The computer then converted this summary score to a letter or number grade that is printed on the report card. Many teachers go on to emphasize the fairness and objectivity of this process, pointing out how the mathematical precision of the computer makes it easy for them to explain and defend their grading policies to students, school leaders, parents, and families.

But do computerized grading programs really make grading fairer and more objective? Or have the technical capabilities of these programs seduced teachers and school leaders into a false sense of confidence in the accuracy and validity of the grades they assign? Have they made it easier for parents and families to track and support their children's learning progress? Or do they persuade parents and families to care more about points and grades than they do about actual learning?

COMPUTERIZED GRADING PROGRAMS

Computerized grading programs and electronic gradebooks rank among the best-selling computer software available to educators today. *Software Advice* currently rates forty-three different computerized grading programs, and numerous other grading programs remain unrated. Many of these programs are extensions of *student information systems* (SIS) developed by software companies to facilitate school record-keeping. They appeal to teachers primarily because they simplify data-recording tasks. The spreadsheet formats and database management systems included in these programs make it easy for teachers to enter and tally large amounts of numerical information (Huber, 1997; Migliorino & Jeffrey, 2004; Vockell & Fiore, 1993). They are particularly well-suited to the point-based grading systems of middle school and high school teachers, who often record numerical data on the performance of more than one hundred students each week.

Most computerized grading programs present teachers with a variety of recording options. Some simply help teachers keep more detailed records on students' learning progress (Eastwood, 1996). Others allow teachers to present summaries of students' performance in a variety of different formats, including computer displays, online reports, and digital portfolios (Lacina, 2012). Still other programs actually perform grading tasks (Srivastava et al., 2020).

Yet for all their advantages, computerized grading programs also have their drawbacks. First, given the current state of the technology and its use, computerized grading programs are far better at supplying information than they are at facilitating communication between school and home (Miller et al., 2016). Second, and perhaps more important, they lead the teachers who use them to believe that mathematical precision brings greater objectivity and enhanced fairness in grading. Many teachers assume that so long as the mathematical calculations are correct and all students are treated the same, then the grades assigned are fair, accurate, and equitable.

> *Computerized grading programs are far better at supplying information than they are at facilitating communication between school and home (Miller et al., 2016).*

> *Numerical precision is not the same as evaluative fairness, honesty, or truth. Likewise, treating all students the same does not make grading equitable.*

What is important to remember, however, is that numerical precision is not the same as evaluative fairness, honesty, or truth. Likewise, treating all students the same does not make grading equitable. While computerized grading programs and electronic gradebooks may simplify record-keeping, they do not lessen the challenge involved in assigning grades that accurately, equitable, and meaningfully reflect students' true level of performance (Guskey, 2002).

THE COMPONENTS OF COMPUTERIZED GRADING PROGRAMS

Although computerized programs vary widely in their features, sophistication, and ease of use, all include three basic components:

1. A gradebook

2. A report card

3. A permanent record or transcript

To use and interpret these components correctly, school leaders and teachers must help parents and families understand the function of these three components and the purpose each is designed to serve (see Table 4.1).

TABLE 4.1   COMPONENTS OF COMPUTERIZED GRADING PROGRAMS

COMPONENT	GRADEBOOK	REPORT CARD	PERMANENT RECORD/ TRANSCRIPT
What does it include?	Scores	Grades	Summary grades
Purpose?	*Ongoing* record of performance	*Interim* summary of performance	*Summary judgments* of performance
Who has access?	Families and students	Families and students	Families, students, and third parties

Gradebook

The gradebook is where teachers record *every* piece of evidence they gather from students. It is an ongoing record of students' performance in school that is updated each time teachers enter new information. In the gradebook, teachers record **scores** from homework assignments, quizzes, formative assessments, compositions, reports, projects, demonstrations, major exams, and summative assessments. Some teachers also record evidence of student behaviors related to tardiness, class participation, punctuality in turning in assignments, and class conduct. Most computerized grading programs allow parents and families access to these data at any time through a parent portal so that they can regularly monitor their child's achievement progress and behavior in school. The majority of programs also allow students to access their own individual records (Hollerbach, 2004).

Report Card

At regular intervals throughout the school year, teachers tally scores and summarize the information they have gathered and recorded on students' performance in the gradebook to determine a marking period *grade*. That grade is then entered on a report card that is made available to parents and families online or on a form that is sent to their home. Most school districts in the United States and Canada use quarterly marking periods where report cards are completed every nine weeks of the school year. Some schools use trimester marking periods, distributing report cards every twelve weeks, while others distribute report cards only at the end of each academic semester, usually after eighteen weeks of classes. Semester report cards are typically accompanied by interim progress reports that are made available online to parents and families or sent home after nine weeks or halfway through each semester.

Teachers vary widely in the procedures they use to determine report card grades. Some schools and school districts have teacher guidelines that stipulate how different kinds of evidence should be weighed in determining report card grades. For example, many schools require that 80 percent of the grade be based on summative evidence and 20 percent based on formative evidence (Pijanowski, 2011). (Note: We will discuss in Chapter 5 the drawbacks of this practice.) But within those categories of evidence, teachers typically have great discretion and significantly differ in the sources of evidence they include (Guskey & Link, 2019). As described in Chapter 3, teachers are more likely to be consistent in the procedures used for determining students' report card grades in schools where staff have collaboratively crafted a purpose statement to guide grading decisions.

> *Teachers are more likely to be consistent in the procedures used for determining students' report card grades in schools where staff have collaboratively crafted a purpose statement to guide grading decisions.*

Permanent Record or Transcript

At the end of the school year, teachers summarize evidence on students' performance gathered over the entire year to determine a *summary grade* in each subject or course that is then recorded on a permanent record or transcript. This summary grade represents teachers' overall evaluation of students' performance for that grade level or course. Again, as we discussed in Chapter 3, what information teachers tally and how they determine that summary grade depends on their determined purpose for grading.

Permanent records typically follow students when families move to other schools or school districts. They provide educators in the new school with a record of students' past performance so that appropriate instructional programs can be planned. At the secondary level, the permanent record becomes a transcript that documents students' high school performance. Transcripts become part of students' college application portfolio and are generally required if students enter military service. They also can be made available to potential employers.

Because third parties (i.e., persons other than students and their parents and families) have access to transcripts, federal and state laws stipulate what they can and cannot include. This is especially important for students with disabilities.

For more informationon on the federal requirements for transcripts, review the details outlined in the U.S. Department of Education's Office of Civil Rights report, *Questions and Answers on Report Cards and Transcripts for Students with Disabilities Attending Public Elementary and Secondary Schools.*

bit.ly/44IX1RL

GRADEBOOKS VERSUS REPORT CARDS

Navigating the different components of computerized grading programs often proves challenging to parents and families, and guidance from school leaders and teachers on how to effectively manage these components can be particularly helpful. One of the most important program features that school leaders and teachers must help parents and families understand is that *not everything recorded in the gradebook is used in determining students' academic report card grades.*

> *Not everything recorded in the gradebook is used in determining students' academic report card grades.*

Gradebooks represent a vital communication tool for teachers to inform parents and families about *all* aspects of students' performance in school. Parents and families should know, for example, if students are completing homework assignments correctly and on time, how they perform on classroom formative assessments, or if they are tardy to class. This information should be recorded in the gradebook, and parents and families should be encouraged to access it regularly through the parent portal in the grading program. This allows them to keep track of their child's learning progress and to intervene immediately when problems or difficulties are evident. Research shows, in fact, that the more frequently parents and families access the online gradebook, the higher the level of students' achievement (Brown, 2014). Frequent access of online gradebook data by students also has been shown to enhance student motivation and self-regulation skills (Brothen, 1996).

> *The more frequently parents and families access the online gradebook, the higher the level of students' achievement (Brown, 2014).*

But including data on homework, formative assessments, and class attendance in the gradebook doesn't mean these behavioral factors will be included in determining students' academic report card grades. As we will discuss in Chapter 5, the best grading systems report these learning-enabling factors separately on the report card *and* on the transcript (Guskey, 2020). In other words, grades for academic performance should not be tainted by the extraneous influence of these or other behavioral factors. Instead, academic report card grades should only represent teachers' evaluations of how well students have mastered specific academic learning goals.

> *The best grading systems report these learning-enabling factors separately on the report card and on the transcript (Guskey, 2020).*

This separation of achievement from behavior in grading and reporting differs from the personal experiences of most parents and families. Many experienced classes in which *everything* counted as part of the grade. At the end of each grading period, their teachers combined evidence from all these different factors into a single amalgamated grade that merged elements of achievement, attitude, effort, and behavior. The result was what researchers refer to as a "hodgepodge grade" (Brookhart & Nitko, 2008) that is impossible to interpret accurately or meaningfully. Because having these factors reported separately is a new experience for most, school leaders and teachers must help parents and families understand the difference between the

> *School leaders and teachers must help parents and families understand the difference between the all-inclusive evidence in the gradebook and the grades recorded on the report card, and why this difference is important.*

all-inclusive evidence in the gradebook and the grades recorded on the report card, and why this difference is important.

STOP AND REFLECT

- How would you go about framing the rationale for this separation of academic performance and behavioral factors to parents who are accustomed to hodgepodge grading?

REPORT CARDS SUMMARIZE DETAILS OFFERED IN GRADEBOOKS

School leaders and teachers must also help parents and families understand that report card grades represent summaries of the detailed information provided in the gradebook. As such, the gradebook and report card must be used together to get the clearest and most meaningful picture of students' performance.

> *The gradebook and report card must be used together to get the clearest and most meaningful picture of students' performance.*

Teachers determine report card grades by combining and summarizing a variety of sources of evidence on students' performance. As we discussed in Chapter 3, the procedures teachers use to combine that evidence vary depending on the defined purpose of grading. When any collection of evidence is combined and summarized, however, important details are always lost. For example, the average of a set of scores doesn't reveal if all those scores were about the same or if they varied widely. When the average alone is reported, important information about the variation among the scores is lost.

At the same time, it's unnecessary for teachers to replicate the detail of the gradebook on the report card. Doing so makes report cards overly complicated and difficult to interpret. Instead, teachers can refer parents and families to the gradebook for that detail so they may see the specific evidence

> *It's unnecessary for teachers to replicate the detail of the gradebook on the report card. Doing so makes report cards overly complicated and difficult to interpret.*

upon which students' report card grades are based. Research shows that although teachers don't believe online gradebooks should ever replace face-to-face conferences with parents and families, the majority believe they can improve parent–teacher communication (Reid, 2018).

In Chapter 5 we will further describe how teachers involved in standards-based or competency-based grading programs don't need to describe students' performance on individual standards on the report card. That information is more efficiently displayed in the gradebook. The report card provides a summary of that evidence and an overall evaluation of students' performance in a subject area or course.

DISABLING COMPUTERIZED GRADING PROGRAMS' TALLYING FUNCTIONS

Many computerized grading programs include a tallying function that calculates a new grade for students each time the teacher enters new information in the gradebook. This new grade may be labelled *Current Grade, Your Grade Today,* or *GPA* (for grade point average). Program developers explain that this function provides students as well as parents and families with an immediate, up-to-date summary of students' performance. However, evidence indicates it also can produce serious negative effects.

Informal surveys conducted in several school districts by the education survey company Grading Rx show that when this function is enabled, parents, families, and students use their phones multiple times each day to access the information. They want to know immediately how any newly entered data affects students' grades. Inadvertently, this function causes parents, families, and students to focus more on points and grades, and less on learning. All attention centers on whether the new data has raised or lowered students' subject or course grades. It makes students reluctant to try new things or explore new endeavors because not doing well causes an immediate reduction in their grade. It also makes teachers hesitant to enter new data, especially when students initially struggle with difficult tasks.

Some teachers try to get around these negative effects by entering the data but then checking *Exclude from the Grade* or assigning a zero weight to the evidence so that it is not immediately tallied. But, again, informal survey data indicate that many parents and families don't understand what these indicators mean or why they are used. The simpler and more effective way to eliminate these negative effects is simply to disable or deactivate this function within the grading program.

Disabling this function frees students to try new approaches and take on new challenges without fearing it will cause irreparable damage to their grade. It allows teachers to help students recognize that making mistakes can be an important part of the learning process, and that what is important is to learn from your mistakes. It also helps parents and families to understand that school is about gaining new insights and learning new things rather than just "getting a grade."

In all classes, teachers should communicate to parents and families how grades will be determined and what evidence counts. A clear purpose statement for grading helps tremendously in this process. But no grade for a report card should be tallied by a grading program before the teacher deter-

> *No grade for a report card should be tallied by a grading program before the teacher determines that it is time.*

mines that it is time. Detailed explanations to parents and families from school leaders and teachers describing the rationale behind these procedures facilitates understanding and usually generates support.

STOP AND REFLECT

- Since many, if not most, parents were led to believe by their experiences that accumulating points and earning good grades is the goal of school, how would you change their thinking without relying on logical argument and personal persuasion alone?

SUMMARY

All computerized programs include three basic components: (1) a gradebook, (2) a report card, and (3) a permanent record or transcript. To use and interpret these components correctly, school leaders and teachers must help parents and families understand the functions of these three components and the purpose each is designed to serve. Parents and families must also be encouraged to understand that the gradebook is an important communication tool that teachers use to share *all* the evidence they gather on every aspect of students' performance in school. But while all this evidence is important, not all is used in determining students' academic achievement grades.

The communication purposes of computerized grading programs are further enhanced when school leaders and teachers help parents and families use the gradebook to clarify the meaning of report card grades and how those grades were determined. However, the immediate tallying functions of computerized grading programs that compute grades for students as soon as new information is recorded in the gradebook *must* be disabled in order to ensure the focus of parents, families, and students remains on learning rather than on accumulating points and getting a grade.

REFERENCES

Brookhart, S. M., & Nitko, A. J. (2008). *Assessment and grading in classrooms*. Pearson Education.

Brothen, T. (1996). A student-accessible computerized gradebook that facilitates self-regulated study behavior. *Teaching of Psychology, 23*(2), 127–130.

Brown, L. D. (2014). *The impact of the usage of electronic grade books on student achievement and parental satisfaction* [Unpublished doctoral dissertation]. Walden University, Minneapolis, MN. https://www.proquest.com/openview/ae4bc0e948051ee57aaa4bb368 84e40b/1?pq-origsite=gscholar&cbl=18750

Eastwood, K. W. (1996). Reporting student progress: One district's attempt with student literacy. In T. R. Guskey (Ed.), *Communicating student learning. 1996 yearbook of the association for supervision and curriculum development* (pp. 65–78). ASCD.

Guskey, T. R. (2002). Computerized gradebooks and the myth of objectivity. *Phi Delta Kappan, 83*(10), 775–780.

Guskey, T. R. (2020). Breaking up the grade. *Educational Leadership, 78*(1), 41–46.

Guskey, T. R., & Link, L. J. (2019). Exploring the factors teachers consider in determining students' grades. *Assessment in Education: Principles, Policy & Practice, 26*(3), 303–320.

Hollerbach, K. (2004). It's a brave new online world. *Phi Kappa Phi Forum, 84*(4), 40+. *Gale Academic OneFile.* link.gale.com/apps/doc/A126195951/AONE?u=anon~798bdd ab&sid=googleScholar&xid=e13467d6

Huber, J. (1997). Gradebook programs: Which ones make the grade? *Technology Connection, 4*(1), 21–23.

Lacina, J. (2012). Technology in the classroom: Virtual record keeping: Should teachers keep online grade books? *Childhood Education, 82*(4), 252–254.

Migliorino, N. L., & Jeffrey, M. (2004). Educator attitudes toward electronic grading software. *Journal of Research on Technology in Education, 36*(3), 193–212.

Miller, R. G., Brady, J. T., & Izumi, J. T. (2016). Stripping the wizard's curtain: Examining the practice of online grade booking in K–12 schools. *School Community Journal, 26*(2), 45–69.

Office of Civil Rights. (2020). *Questions and answers on report cards and transcripts for students with disabilities attending public elementary and secondary schools*. U.S. Department of Education. https://www2.ed.gov/about/offices/list/ocr/letters/colleague-qa-20081017.html

Pijanowski, L. (2011). The case of the illogical grades. *Educational Leadership, 69*(3). https://www.ascd.org/el/articles/the-case-of-the-illogical-grades

Reid, M. J. (2018). *A qualitative case study of teachers' perceptions of the impact of the online gradebook in elementary education* [Unpublished doctoral dissertation]. North Central University, Minneapolis, MN. http://www.proquest.com/en-US/products/dissertations/individuals.shtml

Srivastava, K., Dhanda, N., & Shrivastava, A. (2020). An analysis of automated essay grading systems. *International Journal of Recent Technology and Engineering, 8*(6), 5438–5441.

Vockell, E. L., & Fiore, D. J. (1993). Electronic gradebooks: What current programs can do for teachers. *Clearing House, 66*(3), 141–145.

CHAPTER 5

....

KEEP THE REPORT CARD SIMPLE AND FAMILY FRIENDLY

One of the most common mistakes school leaders make when initiating grading reforms is to focus exclusively on the report card. Recognizing that their current report card offers little useful information to parents and families about students' performance in school, they set out to make the report card a better, more comprehensive, and more informative reporting tool.

Unfortunately, not only is this a poor place to begin, but most reform leaders go overboard in the process. The new report card they develop is often a highly detailed, multiple-page form that overwhelms parents and families with information they don't understand and don't know how to use. This is especially common in reform efforts involving standards-based or competency-based approaches to learning. While adaptations to the report card are essential, the primary goal should be better communication that helps guide improvements in student learning.

KEEP IT SIMPLE

The basic purpose of all standards-based or competency-based learning models is to guarantee *transparency* in all elements of the teaching and learning process: curriculum, instruction, assessment, and reporting. These elements must be clear, concise, and well aligned.

In curriculum, these approaches require the articulation of *clear learning goals that identify what students should learn (content) and be able to do (cognitive*

> **Effective learning goals require both content and process.**

behaviors or processes). Effective learning goals require *both* content and process. In other words, they must specify what students are expected to do with the content they are learning. For example, should students simply be able to remember or recall important content (knowledge)? Or should they be able to explain it in their own words (comprehension), to transfer and use it in a new context (application), to compare or contrast it with related concepts (analysis), or to integrate it with other important ideas (synthesis) (see Bloom et al., 1956). Once made clear, these learning goals must be shared with everyone involved: students, parents and families, teachers, school leaders, and community members.

In most cases, learning goals are organized by grade levels at the elementary level and by courses at the secondary level. But organizational structures associated with continuous progress, learning progressions, individualized programs, or personalized learning can be equally valid.

> **Clear learning goals bring meaning to discussions about curriculum rigor, college and career readiness, and global citizenship.**

Clear learning goals bring meaning to discussions about curriculum rigor, college and career readiness, and global citizenship They clarify the difference between memorizing factual information and developing enduring understandings. An emphasis on essential questions similarly shifts the focus to developing deeper, more complex, and higher-level cognitive skills.

> **Instructionally, educators implementing standards-based or competency-based learning must develop instructional activities that help all students achieve those learning goals.**

Instructionally, educators implementing standards-based or competency-based learning must *develop instructional activities that help all students achieve those learning goals.* This is where discussions of students' entry-level skills, students' interests, cultural relevance, learning modalities, differentiated instruction, project-based learning, cooperative learning, online learning opportunities, flipped classrooms, and alternative forms of instruction become especially important.

> **For assessments, standards-based or competency-based educators must identify what evidence best reflects students' achievement of those learning goals.**

For assessments, standards-based or competency-based educators must *identify what evidence best reflects students' achievement of those learning goals.* This integrates important issues related to formative and summative assessment, assessments *of* and *for* learning, multiple ways for students to demonstrate mastery, authentic and performance-based assessments, meaningful feedback, and student self-regulation, agency, and efficacy.

Finally, standards-based or competency-based learning requires educators to *use grading and reporting strategies that meaningfully communicate students' achievement of those learning goals.* This brings attention to report card and transcript design; reporting on citizenship, work habits, life skills, and other noncognitive skills; and grading and reporting policies and practices.

Standards-based or competency-based learning simply requires transparency and consistency in these elements. It guarantees there is clarity and precision in what we teach, how we teach it, how we evaluate student learning, and how we report students' learning progress.

GRADING AND REPORTING COME LAST

Reform initiatives that have the greatest success address the elements of curriculum, instruction, assessment, and reporting *in order.* They first clarify the learning goals then move to planning how best to teach those goals. They next consider how those goals will be assessed. And finally they turn to grading and reporting student achievement. Attempting to reform grading policies and practices *without* first clarifying crucial aspects of curriculum, instruction, and assessment is a sure ticket to disaster. It typically leads to frustration, inconsistent implementation, and eventual abandonment of reform efforts.

Attempting grading reforms without first addressing these other elements is like trying to put the roof on a house before constructing the foundation and building the walls. The central purpose of transparency in reporting is lost if we are not clear in what we are being transparent about. Critical issues regarding what

> *Standards-based or competency-based learning requires educators to use grading and reporting strategies that meaningfully communicate students' achievement of those learning goals.*

> *Attempting to reform grading policies and practices without first clarifying crucial aspects of curriculum, instruction, and assessment is a sure ticket to disaster.*

> *Critical issues regarding what we teach, how we teach it, and how we assess learning must be addressed before considering how best to grade and report student learning progress*

we teach, how we teach it, and how we assess learning must be addressed before considering how best to grade and report student learning progress in implementing standards-based or competency-based learning models.

BEGIN WITH *WHY,* NOT *WHAT*

After establishing transparency in curriculum, instruction, and assessments, reform leaders can more effectively turn their attention to aspects of grading and reporting. As described earlier, many focus on modifying the report card's structure and changing how report card grades are determined. Others simply adopt the standards-based grading option within their computerized grading program and organize professional learning experiences for teachers on how to use it. Eventually they develop plans to inform parents and families of the changes in grading and reporting they plan to implement.

What these reform leaders often fail to recognize, however, is that the initial concerns of most stakeholders about grading and reporting are not so much about *what* is changing but *why* it needs to change. Parents and families especially often don't see the problems in grading and reporting that reform leaders consider obvious. For example, most don't understand what is wrong with the current report card and related grading policies. After all, the current report card looks much the same as the one they received when they were in school. Even though parents and families may not know exactly how teachers determined the report card grades, they believe they understand what those grades mean.

> *The initial concerns of most stakeholders about grading and reporting are not so much about what is changing but why it needs to change.*

Successful reform leaders *always* begin with *why* before addressing *what.* They offer specific reasons for the changes they want to make before explaining the precise nature of those changes. As we described in Chapter 3, beginning with a clear purpose statement for grading and then showing how current policies and practices don't align with that purpose often proves both informative and highly effective.

> *Successful reform leaders always begin with why before addressing what.*

Parents and families are generally reasonable people who sincerely want what is best for their children. They trust current grading policies and practices because they don't see anything wrong with them. Providing parents and families with a sound rationale for change and specific evidence on the expected improvements tremendously enhances their openness to and acceptance of reforms.

Especially important is a focus on better communication between school and home that will then serve to improve students' learning success (Muñoz & Guskey, 2015).

Several years ago, a group of school district leaders from Kentucky contacted two colleagues and me for assistance in their grading reform efforts and especially in revising their report card. (see Swan et al., 2014). Two of the districts were already well along in the process. They had developed standards-based report cards for kindergarten through fifth grade and wanted to extend their work to the middle school and high school levels. Because the standards at each grade level differed, the report card they developed for every grade level was unique. Each was a highly detailed, multi-page form that listed the standards for every subject area at that grade level. The report card for one particular grade level listed thirty-eight language arts standards and twenty-seven mathematics standards.

Reviewing their work, we found these new report cards extremely difficult to interpret and believed that parents and families might as well. To guide further revisions, we conducted an informal survey of parents and families in each district, asking, "How many ways can student learning in a subject area be sub-divided in order to be more meaningful to you?" We explained this applied to all subjects including language arts, mathematics, physical education, art, etc. The response options offered were (2 or 3), (4 to 6), (7 to 10), (11 to 20), and (More than 20).

The parents and families who responded to the survey were remarkably consistent in their answers: The vast majority chose (4 to 6). Similar surveys conducted in different school districts in different states obtained similar results (see Grading Rx QR code for more information). This confirmed our belief that the current standards-based report cards developed in these districts were overly detailed and far too complex.

Grading Rx
https://gradingrx.com/

HOW TO SUMMARIZE EVIDENCE ON THE REPORT CARD?

The challenge was then to determine how best to summarize evidence on different aspects of student learning on the report card. Our initial thought was to develop broader and more inclusive *essential* standards (DuFour et al., 2010;

Jakicic, 2017), *priority* standards (Ainsworth, 2013, 2015; Spearman, 2020), or *power* standards (Ainsworth, 2003; Reeves, 2007). But as we searched the essential, priority, and power standards developed by different school districts and by different states, we found little consistency or agreement. The developing organizations not only listed different essential, priority, or power standards, they also described different defining characteristics for each.

Seeking a better solution, we tuned to the professional organizations of teachers in each academic discipline. These organizations have all developed detailed standards for student learning in their respective disciplines. (See the corresponding QR code for each organization below.) Furthermore, they have categorized those standards into academic *strands* or *domains*. These strands seemed an excellent way to organize and then summarize students' learning on the report card.

NCTE
bit.ly/3rSaWq6

NCTM
bit.ly/3OGYp1u

NSTA
bit.ly/3rSnGx4

NCSS
bit.ly/3KnFfvf

The professional organizations we considered included:

- National Council of Teachers of English (NCTE), https://ncte.org/

- National Council of Teachers of Mathematics (NCTM) https://www .nctm.org /

- National Science Teaching Association (NSTA), https://www.nsta.org/

- National Council for the Social Studies (NCSS), https://www .socialstudies.org/

- American Council on the Teaching of Foreign Languages (ACTFL), https:// www.actfl.org/

- National Art Education Association (NAEA), https://www.arteducators .org/

- National Association for Music Education (NAME), https://nafme.org/

- Society for Health and Physical Educators (SHAPE), https://www .shapeamerica.org/

In work involving international schools, we also considered the work of the American Education Reaches Out program, Project AERO. Supported by the U.S. State Department's Office of Overseas Schools and the Overseas Schools Advisory Council, this project identifies critical areas of learning in each subject area.

ACTFL
bit.ly/453QVLK

- Project AERO, http://projectaero.org/

In every case, these professional organizations have organized standards for their academic discipline into strands of domains, usually five or six in number. The labels for these strands were developed by experts in that discipline and provided the clarity and consistency we sought. We used these strand labels to summarize student learning on the report card, occasionally modifying a label to make it more understandable and parent-friendly.

NAEA
bit.ly/3OidFAH

NAME
bit.ly/47dUH6Z

Reporting by subject area strands allowed teachers to meaningfully summarize students' performance on the report card without duplicating the information about students' mastery of individual learning standards reported in the gradebook. So instead of reporting on thirty-eight individual language arts standards on the report card, teachers summarized students' learning in language arts in the areas of reading, writing, listening, speaking, and language skills (e.g., grammar, punctuation, spelling, etc.). For detail on the specific standards addressed in each strand, teachers simply referred parents and families to the gradebook, as we discussed in Chapter 4.

SHAPE
bit.ly/3OEu9V0

AERO
bit.ly/3OIsrlS

Another practical advantage in reporting by subject area strands is that while the standards for student learning change with each grade level, the strands do not. Hence, the same report card can be used across *all* elementary grade levels. This greatly simplified report card interpretation for parents and families, who no longer needed to adapt to and interpret a new report card every year.

The differences between gradebook *standards* and report card *strands* are summarized in Table 5.1 below.

TABLE 5.1   DIFFERENCES IN REPORTING

GRADEBOOK *STANDARDS*	REPORT CARD *STRANDS*
Designed to describe all aspects of students' learning	Designed to summarize students' performance
Many in number (ten to fifty per subject)	Relatively few in number (usually four to six per subject)
Highly specific	Broad and more general
Complex and detailed	Clear and understandable
Expressed in subject-specific language	Expressed in parent-friendly language

Reporting summaries of students' performance in subject area strands made the report card a much simpler document that was far easier for parents and families to interpret than the reporting form previously used in these districts. An example of the language arts section of the new report card for Grade 2 is shown in Figure 5.1. As described in Chapter 2, including teachers' photographs on the report card is an idea we borrowed from report card examples we found in several Canadian schools.

STOP AND REFLECT

- If you are a school leader, draft an explanation of the new report card format depicted in Figure 5.1, beginning with your *why* statement. In doing so, be sure to think about the full demographic range of parents and families in your school or district.

- If you are a teacher, how might you walk a parent or family member through this new format in a face-to-face or online meeting? Be sure to keep in mind the differing needs and perspectives of parents across different demographic groups.

Kentucky

STANDARDS BASED REPORT
Elementary Report Card
Student: Chris
Reporting Period: 3

Standard Marks		
4	Exemplary	
3	Proficient	
2	Progressing	
1	Struggling	
N/A	Not Assessed	
*Based on modified standard(s). See Progress Report		

Process Marks	
+ +	Consistently
+	Moderately
–	Rarely
N/A	Not Assessed

Grade 2 Language Arts – Mr. Guskey

Reading	4
Writing	3
Speaking	2
Listening	3
Language	4

Process Goals	
Preparation	+
Participation	+ +
Homework	+
Cooperation	+
Respect	+ +

Description/Comments:

Students have been very busy during the 3rd reporting period working on the following topics: consonants, vowels, and their corresponding sounds; identifying syllables in words; stressed and unstressed syllables; closed syllables, vocabulary development; compound words, antonyms; homophones; synonyms, multiple meaning words; idioms; comprehension skills; main ideas and supporting details; fluency; and reading strategies such as sequencing, cause and effect, and facts and opinions. We also worked on how to answer open-response questions.

Chris is improving with the articulation difficulties that we recently observed. We are coordinating efforts with the speech therapist to continue the progress we've made into the next marking period.

To further clarify the specific skills addressed during the marking period, the report card we developed included a "Description/Comments" section with two parts. The first part contains *class comments* where the teacher enters three or four sentences describing the specific skills students worked on during the quarter. To optimize efficiency, teachers need to enter this information only one time, and those same sentences are printed on the report card of every student in the class. The second part is *student comments* where teachers enter one or two sentences describing each individual student's learning progress. For further explanation, the teacher can refer parents and families to the details recorded in the gradebook.

Remember, however, that the report card does not replace the gradebook; nor can the gradebook replace the report card. Each serves its own special purpose. The report card offers a summary and interim evaluation by teachers of students' perfor-

> *The report card does not replace the gradebook; nor can the gradebook replace the report card.*

mance *at that time* in the school year. Parents and families want to know if their children are on track for success and, if not, what specific improvements are needed. Gradebooks provide the detailed evidence upon which teachers base their interim evaluations and provide the specifics needed to target improvement efforts.

- Isolate two or three stands from one of the national organizations. If you are a teacher, the strand should match your grade level and/or subject area. In parent-friendly language, draft a "class comment" describing the specific skills students worked on during the marking period.

- Next, how might you frame student comments for a student who is considered to be "struggling" with respect to a specific standard?

Although the report card described here offers many advantages, it should not be taken as an exemplary model that other schools or school districts should emulate. Rather, it is but one example of an approach to report card development used by a group of committed educators that was well-received and proved successful for them (see Guskey et al., 2011). Modifications and adaptations to better fit the needs of individual schools and the students they serve are sure to result in improvements that will make report cards far better.

SUMMARY

Report card design is much more a challenge in effective communication than it is about documenting and quantifying students' achievement. Those who take on this challenge must focus primarily on clarity, understanding, and the usefulness of the information provided rather than on its detail and comprehensiveness. To be an effective communication tool, the report card should include information that is clear to parents and families, be easy to understand, and be useful in collaborative efforts to help students improve. If the report card overwhelms parents and families with overly detailed information that they don't fully understand and don't know how to use, that primary communication purpose is lost.

To be an effective communication tool, the report card should include information that is clear to parents and families, be easy to understand, and be useful in collaborative efforts to help students improve.

In addition, report cards should not create bookkeeping nightmares for teachers that require them to duplicate information already available to parents and families in the gradebook. Instead, report cards should communicate teachers' summary judgments of students' performance during the reporting period, as specified in the purpose statement for grading (see Chapter 3). Using the report card in combination with the gradebook reduces the reporting burden for teachers while giving parents and families the information they need to follow their children's progress in school and to guide improvements when needed.

> *Report cards should communicate teachers' summary judgments of students' performance during the reporting period, as specified in the purpose statement for grading*

REFERENCES

Ainsworth, L. (2003). *Power standards: Identifying the standards that matter the most.* Advanced Learning Press.

Ainsworth, L. (2013). *Prioritizing the common core: Identifying specific standards to emphasize the most.* Houghton Mifflin Harcourt.

Ainsworth, L. (2015, February 25). *Priority standards: The power of focus.* Education Week Blog. https://www.edweek.org/teaching-learning/opinion-priority-standards-the-power-of-focus/2015/02

Bloom, B. S., Englehart, M. D., Furst, E. J., Hill, W. H., & Krathwohl, D. R. (1956). *Taxonomy of educational objectives, Handbook 1: The cognitive domain.* McKay.

DuFour, R., Eaker, R., & Many, T. (2010). *Learning by doing: A handbook for professional learning communities at work* (2nd ed.). Solution Tree.

Guskey, T. R., Swan, G. M., & Jung, L. A. (2011). Grades that mean something: Kentucky develops standards-based report cards. *Phi Delta Kappan, 93*(2), 52–57.

Jakicic, C. (2017, May 22). Are essential standards a part of the assessment process? *All Things Assessment, Solution Tree.* http://allthingsassessment.info/2017/05/22/essential-standards-and-the-assessment-process/

Muñoz, M. A., & Guskey, T. R. (2015). Standards-based grading and reporting will improve education. *Phi Delta Kappan, 96*(7), 64–68.

Reeves, D. B. (2007). Power standards: How leaders add value to state and national standards. In Josey-Bass Publishers, *The Jossey-Bass reader on educational leadership* (2nd ed., pp. 239–248). Jossey-Bass.

Spearman, M. M. (2020, July). *Priority standards.* South Carolina Department of Education. https://ed.sc.gov/instruction/career-and-technical-education/programs-and-courses/priority-standards/

Swan, G., Guskey, T. R., & Jung, L. A. (2014). Parents' and teachers' perceptions of standards-based and traditional report cards. *Educational Assessment, Evaluation and Accountability, 26* (3), 289–299.

CHAPTER 6

....

CONSIDER HOW PARENTS AND FAMILIES INTERPRET LABELS

Recall in Chapter 3 we described grades as symbols that educators assign to individual pieces of student work or to composite measures of student performance created for report cards and other summary documents (Guskey & Brookhart, 2019). As such, grades can be letters, numbers, words, symbols, or any set of descriptors that designate different levels of student performance.

Many grading reform initiatives, especially those involving standards-based or competency-based learning models, abandon letter or number grades and instead use words or phrases to describe different student performance levels. This change stems from the belief that grades and numbers carry a certain stigma that may be detrimental to students' self-concept and motivation (Trautwein et al., 2006). By changing the labels used to designate different levels of student performance, reform leaders hope to remove that stigma or at least lessen the negative effects often attributed to letter and number grades. Currently, however, no reliable research studies verify that simply changing labels yields such results.

DOES CHANGING LABELS ALTER PARENTS' AND FAMILIES' INTERPRETATION?

Some evidence on the effects of changing performance level labels came from the early years of education reform in Kentucky. As part of their reform efforts, many elementary schools in the state abandoned the use of letter or number grades. School leaders and teachers in these schools believed that such grades might be harmful to younger students who were just becoming acclimated to school academically and behaviorally. In place of letter and number grades, most schools chose to use the labels developed for the Kentucky state assessment system, which classified student performance in four categories: *Novice*, *Apprentice*, *Proficient*, and *Distinguished*. (Note: Personally, I have always been troubled by the choice of these labels simply because they mix parts of speech: Two are nouns and two are adjectives!)

Several years after the elementary schools made this change, we conducted informal, anonymous surveys of parents and families in several school districts to determine how the change had affected their interpretation of grading and of students' report cards. When asked about their understanding of the new labels, nearly all the parents and families who responded said they made a simple translation: *Distinguished* = A, *Proficient* = B, *Apprentice* = C, *Novice* = D or F. In other words, changing the labels did not alter their interpretation of grades in any way. To modify the way parents and families perceive and interpret grades apparently requires far more than simply changing the names of the labels used.

DO LABELS MATTER?

As a follow-up to this work, colleagues and I set out to determine if the actual words or phrases educators use to describe different levels of student performance make a difference to parents and families. Through an extensive online search of assessment programs, grading programs, proficiency scales, and scoring rubrics, we collected the list of words and phrases displayed in Table 6.1 below. We then grouped these descriptors into five broad categories based on the qualities described, recognizing that *Levels of Understanding* and *Levels of Mastery* may not be clearly distinct.

As the table shows, most scales include four levels of student performance. Educators in the U.S. and Canada generally consider three levels to be insufficient in distinguishing important differences in students' performance. When the number of levels climbs to five or six, however, the consistency of teachers' ratings diminishes rapidly.

To determine how parents and families regard and interpret these labels, another informal, anonymous online survey was conducted asking parents

TABLE 6.1 STUDENT PERFORMANCE LEVEL LABELS

1. LEVELS OF UNDERSTANDING / QUALITY			
Modest	Beginning	Novice	Unsatisfactory
Intermediate	Progressing	Apprentice	Needs
Proficient	Adequate	Proficient	Improvement
Superior	Exemplary	Distinguished	Satisfactory
			Outstanding

2. LEVELS OF MASTERY OF MASTERY / PROFICIENCY			
Below Basic	Below Standard	Pre-emergent	Incomplete
Basic	Approaching Standard	Emerging	Limited
Proficient	Meets Standard	Acquiring	Partial
Advanced	Exceeds Standard	Extending	Thorough

3. FREQUENCY OF DISPLAY		4. EVIDENCE OF ACCOMPLISHMENT	
Rarely	Never	Little or No Evidence	
Occasionally	Seldom	Partial Evidence	
Frequently	Usually	Sufficient Evidence	
Consistently	Always	Extensive Evidence	

5. DEGREE OF EFFECTIVENESS			
Ineffective	Poor		
Moderately Effective	Acceptable		
Highly Effective	Excellent		

and families their impression of the words and phrases included in the table. Specifically, the survey stated:

> *These terms and phrases are used by educators to describe different levels of student performance and achievement. Please mark each with the following:*
>
> *'X' if you think it is clear and informative.*
>
> *'O' if you think it is vague and imprecise.*
>
> *'Blank' if you have no specific opinion.*

Results were analyzed by comparing response frequencies to each word or phrase.

When considering the terms or phrases believed to be clear and informative, responses varied widely. No particular terms or phrases were selected by a majority of parents and families. However, when asked about those believed to be vague and imprecise, two terms or phrases were consistently chosen by large portions of responding parents and families.

First were the terms *Pre-emerging* and *Emerging*. In follow-up interviews, parents and families indicated that rather than a level of student achievement, these terms evoked mental images of "a slimy creature rising from a swamp." When told that *Emerging* generally describes early development or beginning stages, their usual response was, "Then why not use *Beginning*?"—a response we considered both valid and appropriate.

The second phrase consistently rated as vague and imprecise by parents and families was *Exceeds Standard*. This was surprising because *Exceeds* may be the most common of all labels used to describe the highest level of performance in standards-based and competency-based grading reform models.

WHY THE LABEL *EXCEEDS* DOES NOT WORK

When educators identify different levels of student performance, most find the greatest challenge to be defining and labeling the highest performance level. Some believe this should designate a truly exceptional level of achievement: the student whose performance "knocks your socks off." They want to reserve this level to recognize those rare instances when a student does something exceedingly well, truly "wows" the teacher, or performs at a level well beyond what was expected.

Others believe the highest level should describe student performance at a more advanced or more complex cognitive level (see Hoegh et al., 2020). They use the label *Exceeds* to indicate the student has gone beyond the standard and achieved at a higher cognitive level than the standard describes. But while these explanations seem reasonable, serious communication problems arise when educators try to clarify the meaning of *Exceeds Standard* to students, parents and families, and even fellow educators.

Many parents and families consider the label *Exceeds Standard* to be vague, unclear, and difficult to interpret. The message it implies to them from educators is, "More than we expect, but we cannot tell you precisely what that is until we see it!" Such imprecision troubles parents and families, especially those who encourage their child to strive for the highest achievement level and highest grade possible in every subject.

> *Many parents and families consider the label* Exceeds Standard *to be vague, unclear, and difficult to interpret.*

- Choose a standard for any subject area/grade level and discuss how there are many ways to exceed that standard and many interpretations of what that would look like that make it difficult for parents and families to understand. Consider how *Exceeds* may or may not be *Exemplary* or *Distinguished* performance. If you are engaging in this activity as a team, compare your response to others on the team. If there is variance among your responses, discuss the possible reasons for these differing interpretations.

From a practical perspective, *Exceeds Standard* presents additional difficulties. In most standards-based or competency-based environments, mastering a standard means hitting the target and accomplishing what was required. It signifies achieving the specified goal and learning what was expected. Archery offers an fitting example. In Olympic archery, archers attempt to hit the center bulls-eye of a target from a distance of seventy meters. Those who do have achieved the goal and accomplished precisely what was expected.

How then could an Olympic archer ever exceed that standard? How would the archer achieve at a more advanced or higher level? Some might suggest that we could make the center bulls-eye smaller or move the target further away from the archer, making it more difficult to hit the bulls-eye.

The problem with that, however, is it changes the standard. As soon as you make the task more difficult or move the learning expectation to a higher and more advanced level, you have changed the standard and altered the goal. Students who achieve at that level have not really exceeded the standard. More precisely, they have mastered *a different standard*. If you want Olympic archers to hit smaller bulls-eyes from a greater distance, then that becomes the new standard for archers.

> *As soon as you make the task more difficult or move the learning expectation to a higher and more advanced level, you have changed the standard and altered the goal.*

Some suggest that *Proficient* could imply getting near the bulls-eye, while *Exceeds Standard* means actually hitting the bulls-eye directly. But does *Proficient* then mean almost hitting the target? Is getting close sufficient? And if it is, then how close is good enough? Who makes that decision?

This interpretation problem also affects educators who want to equate this distinction to "percent correct" scores on assessments. For example, on an assessment designed to measure students' ability to solve single-digit addition problems, they might designate students who get 80 percent of the problems correct to be *Proficient*, while those students who answer 90 percent or more correctly are rated *Exceeds Standard*. But did the students who got 90 percent correct truly exceed the standard?

Some believe that the assessment for this standard should include double-digit addition problems as well. Students who answer the single-digit *and* double-digit problems correctly can then accurately be rated as *Exceeds Standard*. But again, this miscommunicates what is being measured. With the inclusion of double-digit addition problems, the assessment clearly measures a different standard. The same holds true if *Proficient* requires students to apply or transfer what they have learned, while *Exceeds Standard* involves the higher-level skills of analyzing or synthesizing. The point is that you are now measuring a different standard.

The nature of the specific standard makes things even more complicated. For example, if the standard relates to a student's ability to safely cross a busy street, would anyone consider 80 percent to be *Proficient*? Or even 90 percent? What about being honest or telling the truth? And in these examples, how could students ever reach *Exceeds Standard*?

> A grade that denotes truly distinguished performance can be useful in many instances. But if it is included in the grading system, then that grade must be accompanied by clear criteria that identify precisely how it can be achieved.

This does not imply that exceptional performance should go unrecognized. A grade that denotes truly distinguished performance can be useful in many instances. But if it is included in the grading system, then that grade must be accompanied by clear criteria that identify precisely how it can be achieved. Those criteria must be communicated to students and parents and families alike. Understanding is further enhanced if these criteria can be accompanied by illustrative examples of students' performance or samples of students' work.

With these criteria articulated and clearly communicated to all stakeholders— students, parents and families, fellow teachers, and school leaders—labels such as *Distinguished*, *Exceptional*, or *Exemplary* generally serve intended communication purposes far better than *Exceeds Standard*. (see Guskey, 2014).

IMPLICATIONS FOR DEVELOPING RUBRICS

This same reasoning also applies to the development of rubrics. Susan Brookhart (2013) defines a rubric as "a coherent set of criteria for students' work that includes descriptions of levels of performance quality on the criteria" (p. 4). Rubrics help educators describe and offer feedback on student performance at all levels of education. Recently, however, educators have come under fire for the way they translate rubric scores to grades on report cards. Although many believe the problem lies with grades, closer analysis reveals the real problem is the way we construct the rubrics.

Most educators begin developing rubrics by articulating what students must learn and be able to do to meet a standard or be *Proficient*. From there they identify two or three levels leading up to *Proficient* to describe students' progress, and then they designate one level above to recognize higher or more complex learning. This approach tends to work well in elementary grades where higher or more complex learning usually means *Above Grade Level*.

Problems arise, however, when applications extend to the secondary level where students and parents and families have concerns about grades, GPAs, transcripts, and college admissions. The question high school students ask is not, "How do I meet the standard?" Instead, they want to know, "What must I do to achieve the highest level

> *The question high school students ask is not, "How do I meet the standard?" Instead, they want to know, "What must I do to achieve the highest level possible?"*

possible?" Because in most secondary schools that highest level translates to a letter grade, the question then becomes, "What do I need to do to get an *A*?"

Some educators believe this problem can be solved by getting rid of letter grades. But as we discussed earlier in this chapter, letter grades are simply one of a variety of ways to label categories of student performance. Whether those labels are letters, numerals, words, or symbols makes little difference.

Other educators try to change the attitudes of students and their parents and families about grades, exhorting them to focus more on learning and less on the grades. But such efforts rarely succeed. As we described in Chapter 2, attitudes are shaped by experience, and most students' and parents' experience tells them grades are important. In addition, students and parents and families often look ahead to the college application process where, despite recent trends to consider a broader range of student data in granting admission and scholarships, grades still count.

Furthermore, many parents urge their children to strive for the highest level of achievement possible. They may accept the teacher's explanation that the highest level is reserved for truly exceptional performance; that is, work that goes above and beyond the standard. Nevertheless, that remains the level they want their child to achieve, especially if levels are tied to grades. For these parents and families, *Proficient* is not sufficient. They want their child to make every effort to reach whatever level the teacher designates as the highest.

A NEW APPROACH TO DEVELOPING RUBRICS

To solve this problem, educators must change the way they develop rubrics. Specifically, they need to return to the approach recommended by Benjamin Bloom (1968, 1971) in outlining the process of mastery learning (see Guskey, 2023a). Bloom knew that no matter how he defined *mastery*, certain groups would disagree. So he simply turned the question back to teachers.

Nearly all teachers evaluate students' performance and assign grades or marks based on those evaluations. If the grades or marks are criterion-based—that is, based on what students learned and are able to do—then teachers have already identified mastery: It is the level of performance established for a grade of *A*. So rather than press teachers to define *mastery* anew, Bloom simply instructed them, "Tell me what you expect of students to receive a grade of *A*." That level of performance then becomes the learning expectation for all.

As Bloom described in his classic 1968 article, "Learning for Mastery":

> *We are expressing the view that, given sufficient time and appropriate types of help, 95% of students...can learn a subject up to a high level of mastery. We are convinced that the grade of 'A' as an index of mastery of a subject can, under appropriate conditions, be achieved by up to 95% of the students in a class. (p. 4)*

So instead of developing rubrics by starting in the middle and working up and down, we need to start at the top by describing excellent performance and then work down. If that top level represents learning at a higher and more complex level than the standard, then identify clearly what that learning is. What does it look like? What kind of evidence or demonstration shows it? How will the teacher recognize it? If some students and

> *Instead of developing rubrics by starting in the middle and working up and down, we need to start at the top by describing excellent performance and then work down.*

parents and families want to make that level their standard, that's fine. And if *Proficient* is below that, then so be it.

Debates about what level of student performance represents excellence and true mastery are both useful and necessary. These decisions are matters of choice and involve value judgments on the part of educators (see Guskey, 2023b). But those are precisely the decisions educators need to make when they develop rubrics. The frustration of students and their parents and families rarely comes from the rigor of educators' expectations for students' performance. It comes instead from the lack of clarity regarding those expectations and the lack of appropriate support given to students to meet those expectations.

> *The frustration of students and their parents and families rarely comes from the rigor of educators' expectations for students' performance. It comes instead from the lack of clarity regarding those expectations and the lack of appropriate support given to students to meet those expectations.*

Educators must clearly articulate what it means to achieve at the highest level. They must clearly define the criteria used to describe that level of learning and share those criteria with students, parents and families, teaching colleagues, and school leaders. They must identify explicitly what types of evidence reflect that level of achievement and how that evidence will be evaluated. To succeed in grading and reporting reforms, we need to worry less about what label we attach to the highest level of student performance, and more about the

> *To succeed in grading and reporting reforms, we need to worry less about what label we attach to the highest level of student performance, and more about the criteria we use to define it and what we can do to help all students achieve it (Guskey, 2017).*

criteria we use to define it and what we can do to help *all* students achieve it (Guskey, 2017).

SUMMARY

Choosing the labels we use to describe different levels of student performance may seem a simple process, but how parents and families interpret those labels needs to be an essential consideration. Current evidence indicates that while no set of labels is overwhelmingly favored by parents and families, certain labels draw significant criticism due to their ambiguity and lack of specificity. In particular, reform leaders would be wise to avoid the labels *Emerging* and *Exceeds Standard* because of their lack of clarity.

> *While no set of labels is overwhelmingly favored by parents and families, certain labels draw significant criticism due to their ambiguity and lack of specificity.*

Furthermore, school leaders and teachers must be prepared to address the concerns of parents and families who encourage their children to strive for the highest achievement level possible, especially at the middle school and high school levels. This requires a significant change in the procedures used to develop rubrics and performance criteria. Specifically, instead of starting in the middle at *Proficient* and working both down and up, we must begin by first articulating what is expected from students to achieve that highest level. Successful reform leaders ensure those criteria are clear, precise, meaningful, and easy for students and their parents and families to understand. This clarity also provides a foundation for meaningful conversations about the rigor, appropriateness, and validity of those criteria.

REFERENCES

Bloom, B. S. (1968). Learning for mastery. *Evaluation Comment (UCLA-CSIEP)*, 1(2), 1–12.

Bloom, B. S. (1971). Mastery learning. In J. H. Block (Ed.), *Mastery learning: Theory and practice* (pp. 47–63). Holt, Rinehart & Winston.

Brookhart, S. M. (2013). *How to create and use rubrics for formative assessment and grading.* ASCD.

Guskey, T. R. (2014, October 17). *Why the label 'Exceeds Standard' doesn't work.* Education Week Blog. http://blogs.edweek.org/edweek/finding_common_ground/2014/10/why_the_label_exceeds_standard_doesnt_work.html

Guskey, T. R. (2017, February 6). *New direction in the development of rubrics.* Corwin Connect. http://corwin-connect.com/2017/02/new-direction-development-rubrics/

Guskey, T. R. (2023a). *Implementing mastery learning* (3rd ed.). Corwin Press.

Guskey, T. R. (2023b, April 24). *Should curriculum teach students to obey or to improve society?* Education Week Blog. https://www.edweek.org/teaching-learning/opinion-should-curriculum-teach-students-to-obey-or-to-improve-society/2023/04

Guskey, T. R., & Brookhart, S. M. (Eds.). (2019). *What we know about grading: What works, what doesn't, and what's next?* ASCD.

Hoegh, J. K., Heflebower, T., &Warrick, P. B. (2020). *A handbook for developing and using proficiency scales in the classroom.* Marzano Resources.

Trautwein, U., Lüdtke, O., Marsh, H. W., Köller, O., & Baumert, J. (2006). Tracking, grading, and student motivation: Using group composition and status to predict self-concept and interest in ninth-grade mathematics. *Journal of Educational Psychology, 98*(4), 788–806.

CHAPTER 7

....

REPLACE OLD TRADITIONS WITH NEW AND BETTER TRADITIONS

To reform grading and reporting means challenging some of education's longest-held and most firmly entrenched traditions. Many of these traditions have long outlived their usefulness and stifle progress. Although no evidence shows these traditions are effective or serve to enhance the learning experiences of students, they are maintained simply because "We've always done it that way."

Successful reform leaders recognize, however, that traditions have an important role in every society. They are the way we transmit customs, beliefs, or ways of acting from one generation to the next. All traditions have some origin in the past and

> *Challenging time-honored traditions means disrupting the security those traditions provide.*

provide a sense of stability and consistency as we move forward in time. Challenging time-honored traditions means disrupting the security those traditions provide. It means pushing people away from something they find comfortable and familiar and toward a place of uncertainty and anxiety.

Some reform leaders attempt to challenge these traditions through direct confrontation. They describe how certain grading traditions are harmful to students' confidence in themselves as learners, discourage student collaboration, and can damage the relationship between teachers and students. But confrontation rarely succeeds simply because, as we discussed in Chapter 2, it runs counter to the experiences of most stakeholders. Instead of opening minds to other options, it causes discussions of grading reform to degenerate into battles of opposing opinions that divert attention and sabotage change efforts. Research shows that to debate another's opinions often serves only to deepen the other's attachment to those opinions (Shatz, n.d.).

> *To succeed in grading reform, school leaders and teachers must be sensitive to the loss of security, the intense anxiety, and the extreme discomfort that come with abandoning established traditions.*

To succeed in grading reform, school leaders and teachers must be sensitive to the loss of security, the intense anxiety, and the extreme discomfort that come with abandoning established traditions. They must understand the historic importance of these traditions and why they have been maintained despite the lack of substantiating evidence. Most important, reform leaders must be prepared to offer new, evidence-based traditions to take the place of the older traditions being left behind (Guskey, 2020b).

REPLACING THE OLD WITH NEW AND BETTER

As we discussed in Chapter 3, challenging long-held traditions in grading and reporting always must begin with *why* rather than *what*. Parents and families are generally reasonable people who sincerely want what is best for children. They trust current grading policies and practices primarily because they experienced those same policies, practices, and traditions when they were in school and see nothing wrong with them.

School leaders and teachers who want to succeed in grading reforms don't confront parents and families with dissenting opinions that deny their experiences. Instead, they ease parents' and families' concerns by providing a sound rationale for change, a thorough explanation of *why* the change is important, and specific evidence to support the changes they plan to implement. Initially focusing on *why* can greatly improve parents' and families' openness to the proposed reforms. Reform leaders who can offer new traditions that remedy the negative aspects of the old traditions and provide specific benefits to students and their parents and families enhance the chances of success even more.

Four long-held grading and reporting traditions challenged by many reform leaders include the following:

1. Redefining the honor roll
2. Determining students' class rank

3. Selecting the class valedictorian

4. Reporting a single grade for each subject area or class

In this chapter, we consider each of these traditions and why it should be changed. We then offer new traditions to take their place that can bring multiple benefits to students as well as parents and families.

REDEFINING THE HONOR ROLL

Beginning in the early elementary grades, students who achieve high grades in every subject or in all classes during a reporting period are named on the school's honor roll. Although the criteria for getting on the honor roll vary, most schools use either a grade count (i.e., all *As* and *Bs*) or an overall grade point average (GPA).

Some writers on grading issues recommend we do away with honor rolls completely. They argue that honor rolls overemphasize the importance of grades and make learning overly competitive (Sackstein, 2015; Wormeli, 2010). But many school leaders and teachers reject the idea of eliminating honor rolls, insisting that they are a meaningful and time-honored way to recognize students for their academic success.

A more pertinent but often overlooked criticism of honor rolls, however, is the narrowness by which they define *honor*. In nearly all schools, honor rolls recognize academic achievement *only*. True honor, however, is much more than just academic prowess. The many other aspects of honor that greatly influence students' success and sense of fulfillment in school and in their lives beyond school are generally ignored.

> *In nearly all schools, honor rolls recognize academic achievement only. True honor, however, is much more than just academic prowess.*

By definition, *honor* can be a noun or a verb. As a noun it generally means high respect, great esteem, or adherence to what is right, similar to integrity or honesty. As a verb, *honor* means to regard with great respect, to fulfill an obligation, or to keep a promise.

The Girl Scout Promise and the Boy Scout Oath, for example, both begin with the phrase, "On my honor . . ." When either a Girl Scout or Boy Scout makes a solemn pledge, they end with the phrase "Scout's honor" to indicate the highest level of sincerity.

Honor serves as the central value in every branch of the U.S. military. The Honor Code at each of the military academies defines a system of ethics and code of conduct for cadets studying there. The Honor Code at the U.S. Military Academy at West Point, for example, states, "A cadet will not lie, cheat, steal, or tolerate those who do." The oldest and most prestigious recognition that may be awarded to a U.S. military service member is the Medal of Honor.

Yet according to Terry Newell, author of the 2015 best-seller *To Serve with Honor*, the concept of honor has been lost in nearly all professions and especially in public service. He argues that although honor should pervade all of what we do, it is confined today only to those in the military. His book is an impassioned call to restore honor to its needed place in public service and in all aspects of life.

As educators strive to help students develop 21st century skills and become college and career ready, it seems they, too, have lost sight of the importance of honor. We focus on the qualities and characteristics that contribute to a person's professional or financial success, but we neglect what makes that success meaningful. We ignore important questions about whether the means used to gain that success were good, fair, and honest. Is success in any area worth having or a goal worth achieving if we sacrifice our honor and integrity along the way?

So instead of doing away with the tradition of the school honor roll, why not expand the definition of *honor* and make it a core value in every school. Why not build honor into the curriculum and establish it as one of the primary learning goals we want students to achieve? Of course we want students to strive for success and to revel in the recognition that comes from that success. But we also must help students understand that just as important as success is how you gain it. No achievement in any endeavor is worth the sacrifice of your honor and dignity.

A new and better honor roll could reflect not only academic achievement but truly honorable actions by students that show courage and commitment. Those named to the honor roll could be students who make special efforts to include those who are different and students who intervene to prevent someone from being bullied in school or out of school. It could include students who set aside their own self-interests to help other students resolve serious problems or succeed on especially challenging tasks. It could acknowledge students for acts of kindness, generosity, empathy, and civic responsibility. It could recognize students who put others before themselves and champion the cause of social justice.

- Reflect on the students in your classroom or school. What are some examples of nonacademic behaviors, actions, or outcomes that you have heard about or observed that would warrant placing a student on the honor roll?

Broadening the definition of honor would allow schools to move beyond a narrow focus on academic achievement and to consider acts of service and traits like leadership, bravery, compassion, honesty, dependability, and helpfulness. Procedures could be established to encourage students to nominate classmates for the honor roll based on actions of which teachers and school leaders may be unaware. Such procedures would help all students recognize that honorable acts not only contribute to their success in the world today but will guide them in building a better world for tomorrow. Most important, it gives educators a way to recognize students whose selfless acts bring honor to themselves, to their parents and families, and to their schools in the process (Guskey, 2020d, 2022).

DETERMINING STUDENTS' CLASS RANK

Many high schools throughout the U.S. and Canada rank graduating students according to their cumulative grade point average, or GPA. Schools vary widely in the procedures they use to determine students' GPAs. Some high schools, for example, consider grades from all classes, while others include only designated academic classes. Some schools assign equal weight to grades from all classes, while other schools employ complicated weighting strategies that attach higher value to grades attained in courses perceived to be more challenging (Downs, 2000).

A crucial but often unasked question with regard to determining students' class rank is, Why do we do it? Why do high school officials calculate students' GPAs to the hundred-thousandth decimal point in order to ensure accuracy in that ranking? What purpose does ranking graduating students serve?

> *A crucial but often unasked question with regard to determining students' class rank is, Why do we do it?*

Although some states use class rank as a basis for offering merit-based scholarships (Tennessee Higher Education Commission, 2012), a recent

> *In many instances, the process of determining class rank actually hurt students' chances of admission to highly selective colleges and universities (Boccella, 2016).*

report by the National Association for College Admission Counseling (Clinedinst, 2019) indicates that more than half the high schools in the U.S. no longer report students' class rank. Why? Because high-achieving high schools found it penalized many excellent students who were squeezed out of the top 10 percent of the class and then overlooked by elite colleges (College Board, n.d.). In many instances, the process of determining class rank actually hurt students' chances of admission to highly selective colleges and universities (Boccella, 2016).

In addition, a survey by Eric Hoover (2012), senior writer at the Chronicle of Higher Education, found that only 19 percent of colleges and universities say class rank has considerable importance in the application process, and indications are that percentage continues to decline (O'Brien, 2014). Most admissions officers express serious skepticism about the meaningfulness of class rank (McKibben, 2017).

> *The process of determining students' class rank does nothing to improve student achievement or prompt students to attain higher levels of learning.*

It is also important to recognize that the process of determining students' class rank does nothing to improve student achievement or prompt students to attain higher levels of learning. With the possible exception of the top-ranked students, it also does nothing to enhance students' sense of self-worth, their confidence as learners, or their motivation for learning. In fact, evidence indicates that it accomplishes quite the opposite and diminishes students' motivation (Covington, 1992).

If we eliminate the tradition of determining students' class rank, what new and better tradition might we put in its place? An increasing number of high schools are adopting the Latin honor system, similar to that used by colleges and universities, to recognize graduating seniors' academic achievements. In this system, students who earn a cumulative GPA of 3.50 or higher graduate *cum laude*, 3.75 or higher graduate *magna cum laude*, and those at 4.0 graduate *summa cum laude*. In other words, the honor is based on specific achievement criteria rather than students' relative standing among classmates. Students compete against the curriculum; not against each other.

Wilson High School in Reading, Pennsylvania, made this change after hearing from past graduates that they felt victimized by the competition to maintain a higher GPA than their classmates. To them, the determination of class rank made high school a nerve-wracking and unpleasant experience. Under the new policy, Wilson recognizes students for academic achievement measured against a standard of excellence instead of comparing them to their peers (Heesen, 2013).

The response to the change at Wilson High School among students, as well as among parents and families, has been overwhelmingly positive. In describing the change, one high-achieving Wilson student said, "I feel that the new system puts the focus on your education instead of competing for a name." (Heesen, 2013, p. 2). Similar results have been noted in a comparable program implemented at Redmond High School in Redmond, Oregon (Tribune, 2013; see the QR code, above). A criterion-based program like the Latin honor system allows students with exceptional academic achievement to be recognized without the negative aspects associated with competitive, norm-based class ranks (Guskey, 2014).

Redmond High School Results
bit.ly/3QFHDBF

SELECTING THE CLASS VALEDICTORIAN

An issue often related to determining students' class rank is selection of the class valedictorian. In most high schools in the U.S., the student chosen as the class valedictorian is the top-ranked student who attained the highest weighted grade point average. This seemingly innocent process pits students against each other to gain that singular distinction and often results in aggressive and sometimes bitter competition among high-achieving students (Guskey, 2008, 2018b).

Early in their high school careers, top-achieving students analyze the selection procedures used in their school to pick the class valedictorian. Then, often with the help of their parents, they find ingenious ways to improve their standing in comparison to classmates. Gaining the honor does not simply require high achievement; it requires outdoing everyone else in the class. And sometimes the difference among these top-achieving students is as little as one-thousandth of a decimal point in their weighted GPA. Stories abound of students "gaming" the system in order to gain some advantage; friendships among students being ruined because of the fierce competition; and students avoiding classes in art, music, or dance because even an *A* in an unweighted class can bring down their GPA. There are also numerous reports of parents threatening lawsuits because they believed their child was somehow wronged in the process ("Valedictorians: Who Needs Them?" 2012).

Some high schools try to lessen the competition by identifying the top ten ranked students in the class. But while this may ease the tension among those top ten students, it does little for the student ranked eleventh. In addition, the choice of ten is quite arbitrary. Why not twelve? Or twenty? Regardless of the number chosen, the result remains the same. Excellence is not defined by specific, rigorous, and challenging learning criteria. It is defined in terms of a student's relative standing among classmates.

Ironically, the term *valedictorian* has nothing to do with achievement. It comes from the Latin *vale dicere*, which means "to say farewell." It is the individual selected from the graduating class to deliver a farewell address, called a valedictory, at the commencement ceremony. The idea of having a student speaker at commencement exercises is one of most established traditions in all of education. The first reference to valedictorian can be traced to the diary of the Reverend Edward Holyoke, president of Harvard College in 1759, who wanted to include a student among the speakers at the graduation ceremony (Guskey, 2015).

The problems associated with naming the class valedictorian are not resolved by eliminating the tradition and not having a valedictorian. The solution rests in establishing a new tradition that changes the way the valedictorian is selected.

Increasing numbers of high schools are adopting the same procedures used by colleges and universities to select the student commencement speaker or valedictorian (Guskey, 2011). Depending on the institution, high-achieving college or university graduates might vote to determine who will represent them as valedictorian at the commencement ceremony. In some cases, the entire graduating class nominates and then votes for the person who they believe best represents the class ideals. Sometimes the faculty appoints the valedictorian based on a merit system that takes into account not only grades but also involvement in meaningful service projects and extracurricular activities. At some institutions, students compete in an essay contest to give the valedictory speech, while at other schools a committee composed of students and faculty nominates students for the honor.

All educators, as well as all parents and families, champion the idea of acknowledging students' outstanding achievements. They support programs of specific incentives that encourage students to work hard and do their very best. But ranking students based on their cumulative GPA and using that ranking to determine the class valedictorian pits students against each other in virulent competition that can destroy friendships and ruin the school culture.

By maintaining the tradition of having a class valedictorian in order to give students a voice in the graduation ceremony but changing the method used to select the valedictorian, educators can begin a new tradition that offers clear advantages to students and benefits the entire school community.

> *By maintaining the tradition of having a class valedictorian in order to give students a voice in the graduation ceremony but changing the method used to select the valedictorian, educators can begin a new tradition that offers clear advantages to students and benefits the entire school community*

REPORTING MULTIPLE GRADES

Every marking period teachers gather evidence on students' performance from scores attained on major examinations, compositions, projects, and classroom assessments. They record data on students' homework completion, class participation, and punctuality in turning in assignments. Some teachers gather additional information on students' behavior in class, collaboration with classmates, and effort. To determine students' report card grades, they sum across these weighted categories of evidence, determine a cumulative total, and then assign a single overall grade based on that total. The result is an amalgamated "hodgepodge" grade (Brookhart, 1991, p. 36) that is impossible to interpret accurately because it indiscriminately mixes achievement and noncognitive (behavioral) factors that may or may not be related (Guskey, 2018a).

A more useful and far more meaningful description of students' performance includes multiple grades. At a minimum, it provides grades that distinguish *product*, *process*, and *progress* learning criteria.

> *A more useful and far more meaningful description of students' performance includes multiple grades.*

STOP AND REFLECT

- If you are a teacher, do you currently assign a single grade that mixes achievement and behavior or noncognitive factors?

- What are potential barriers to changing your current grading system to one that assigns multiple grades for different criteria?

- If you are a school leader, what are the barriers that could get in the way of a schoolwide shift to multiple grades?

Product criteria reflect how well students have achieved specific learning goals, standards, or competencies. These might be determined by students' performance on major examinations, compositions, projects, reports, or other culminating demonstrations of learning. Product criteria describe students' academic achievements; that is, what they have learned and are able to do as a result of their experiences in school.

Process criteria describe student behaviors that facilitate or broaden learning. These may be things that *enable* learning, such as formative assessments, homework, and class participation. They also may reflect *extended learning* goals related to collaboration, responsibility, communication, perseverance, habits of mind, or citizenship. In some cases, process criteria relate to students' *compliance* with class procedures, such as turning in assignments on time or not interrupting during class discussions.

Progress criteria show how much students have gained or improved. Sometimes these are referred to as "improvement" or "value-added" criteria. Although related to product criteria, progress criteria are distinct. It would be possible, for example, for students to make outstanding progress but still not be meeting course academic goals or achieving at grade level. It also would be possible for highly skilled and talented students to show they have achieved the product criteria without making notable progress or improvement.

Although these types of learning criteria vary in their importance depending on the subject area and grade level, all three are essential to school success. Meaningful communication about that success, however, requires that they be reported separately. In other words, students must receive different grades for whatever product, process, and progress criteria are considered most important in their learning (Guskey, 1996, 2020c).

GRADING CRITERIA

1. Product (achievement of learning goals)

2. Process (behaviors that enable learning)

3. Progress (improvement or learning gain)

Although the idea of reporting multiple grades seems novel to most educators in the U.S., schools throughout Canada have done this for decades. In the province of Ontario, for example, teachers separate achievement grades from the *Learning Skills and Work Habits* of responsibility, organization, independent work, collaboration, initiative, and self-regulation (see QR code). Teachers there indicate that students take these non-cognitive factors more seriously when they are reported separately rather than merged into an overall hodgepodge grade. These multiple grades are recorded on the report card *and* on the transcript.

Ontario Report Card Templates
bit.ly/3rWzJt2

Ironically, reporting multiple grades for these different criteria does not require extra work for teachers. In fact, it turns out to be less work. Teachers already gather evidence on different product, process, and progress criteria. They keep detailed records of students' scores on various measures of achievement, as well as formative assessment results, homework completion, class participation, collaboration in teamwork, etc. By simply reporting separate grades for these different aspects of learning, teachers avoid the dilemmas involved in determining how much each should be weighted in calculating a single grade.

> *Reporting multiple grades for these different criteria does not require extra work for teachers. In fact, it turns out to be less work.*

> *By simply reporting separate grades for these different aspects of learning, teachers avoid the dilemmas involved in determining how much each should be weighted in calculating a single grade.*

Reporting multiple grades on the report card *and* on the transcript further emphasizes to students that these different aspects of their performance are all important. Parents and families gain advantages because the report card now provides a more detailed and comprehensive picture of their children's performance in school. In addition, because product grades are no longer tainted by evidence based on students' behavior or compliance, those grades more closely align with external measures of achievement and content mastery, such as state assessments, AP exam results, and ACT or SAT scores—a quality that college and university admissions officers have been shown to favor.

The biggest challenge for teachers and school leaders in reporting multiple grades rests in determining what particular product, process, and progress criteria to report. This requires careful thinking about the learning criteria that are most important to students' success in school and beyond. From a practical perspective, it also involves finding an acceptable balance between providing enough detail to be meaningful but not so exhaustive that it creates a bookkeeping burden for teachers (Amir & Guskey, 2024).

How teachers and school leaders label these noncognitive process goals on the report card and transcript also turns out to be important to parents and families. Research by Adam Tyner (2021) of the Fordham Institute indicates, for example, that while parents and families want their children to learn important process skills such as collaboration, empathy, goal setting, and understanding differences, they do not like the phrase *social and emotional learning*. The parents and families surveyed also did not respond well to abstract terms like *whole child development* and *soft skills*. Terms such as *life skills, learning skills, work habits*, or *employability skills* are more generally understood and far more acceptable.

In explaining the shift to multiple grades to parents and families, successful reform leaders always begin with *why*. They describe how combining aspects of achievement, behavior, responsibility, and effort into a single grade makes the grade impossible to interpret and diminishes the value of grades in efforts to help students improve (Guskey, 2020a). Many use practical illustrations based on actual data to show how the mindless calculations used in computerized grading programs often falsely depict what students have learned and are able to do (Guskey & Jung, 2016; Rose, 2016). Others explain how including noncognitive factors in determining students' achievement grades leaves educators open to legal challenges contesting the meaning and interpretation of grades (see Link, 2019). Above all, they emphasize that grading is primarily about effective communication rather than simply quantifying achievement, and multiple grades are a crucial component in making that communication accurate, clear, meaningful, and equitable.

SUMMARY

Many long-established school traditions are based on grades. Examples include the honor roll, the determination of students' class rank, procedures for selecting the class valedictorian, and reporting a single grade for each subject area or class. Successful grading reforms are not accomplished by simply abandoning these long-held but outdated traditions. Instead, we must find ways to replace these traditions with new and better ones that are more purposeful and educationally sound. In this chapter we explained why these traditions should be changed and offered new traditions that can be implemented in their place. Although these new traditions do not require a lot of extra work for teachers or school leaders, they offer numerous benefits for students and are likely to win the support of parents and families.

REFERENCES

Amir, A. S. F., & Guskey, T. R. (2024). *Life skills for all learners: How to teach, assess, and report education's new essentials.* ASCD.

Boccella, K. (2016, October 30). More top high schools drop out of class-rank system. *The Philadelphia Inquirer.* http://www.philly.com/philly/education/20161030_More_top_high_schools_drop_out_of_class-rank_system.html

Brookhart, S. M. (1991). Grading practices and validity. *Educational Measurement: Issues and Practice, 10*(1), 35–36.

Clinedinst, M. (2019). *2019 state of college admission.* National Association for College Admission Counseling. https://nacacnet.org/wp-content/uploads/2022/10/soca2019_all.pdf

College Board. (n.d.). *Class rank and college admission.* https://counselors.collegeboard.org/college-application/class-rank

Covington, M. V. (1992). *Making the grade, a self-worth perspective on motivation and school reform.* Cambridge University Press.

Downs, G. C. (2000). *Weighted grades: A conundrum for secondary schools* (Occasional paper no. 35). Center for Research and Evaluation, University of Maine.

Guskey, T. R. (1996). Reporting on student learning: Lessons from the past—Prescriptions for the future. In T. R. Guskey (Ed.), *Communicating student learning. 1996 yearbook of the Association for Supervision and Curriculum Development* (pp. 13–24). Association for Supervision and Curriculum Development.

Guskey, T. R. (2008, April 17). High schools should end valedictorian tradition. *The Lexington Herald-Leader,* A-15.

Guskey, T. R. (2011). Five obstacles to grading reform. *Educational Leadership, 69*(3), 16–21.

Guskey, T. R. (2014). Class rank weights down true learning. *Phi Delta Kappan, 95*(6), 15–19.

Guskey, T. R. (2015). *On your mark: Challenging the conventions of grading and reporting.* Solution Tree.

Guskey, T. R. (2018a, February 4). *Multiple grades: The first step to improving grading and reporting.* Education Week Blog. http://blogs.edweek.org/edweek/leadership_360/2018/02/multiple_grades_the_first_step_to_improving_grading_and_reporting.html

Guskey, T. R. (2018b, May 14). Should schools have valedictorians? *The New York Times Upfront,* 23.

Guskey, T. R. (2020a). Breaking up the grade. *Educational Leadership, 78*(1), 41–46.

Guskey. T. R. (2020b, January 6). *Classic mistakes made in grading reform, and how to avoid them.* Solution Tree Blog. https://www.solutiontree.com/blog/classic-mistakes-in-grading-reform-and-how-to-avoid-them/#more-4936

Guskey, T. R. (2020c). *Get set, go! Creating successful grading and reporting systems.* Solution Tree.

Guskey, T. R. (2020d, March 8). *Isn't it time we redefine honor roll?* Education Week Blog. http://blogs.edweek.org/edweek/finding_common_ground/2020/03/isnt_it_time_we_redefine_honor_roll.html

Guskey, T. R. (2022, May 16). As we calculate success in work and school, let's not forget the concept of honor. *The Lexington Herald-Leader,* A-5. https://www.kentucky.com/opinion/op-ed/article261408177.html

Guskey, T. R., & Jung, L. A. (2016). Grading: Why you should trust your professional judgment. *Educational Leadership, 73*(7), 50–55.

Heesen, B. A. (2013, May 20). Wilson to drop valedictorian distinction; Latin honors system will include more seniors. *Reading Eagle*, 1–2.

Hoover, E. (2012, December 7). High-school class rank, a slippery metric, loses its appeal for colleges. *The Chronicle of Higher Education*, 56(15), A1, A5.

Link, L. J. (2019). Leadership for grading reform. In T. R. Guskey & S. M. Brookhart (Eds.), *What we know about grading: What works, what doesn't, and what's next?* (pp. 157–194). ASCD.

McKibben, S. (2017). Stepping out of rank. *Education Update*, 59(9), 2–3, 6.

Newell, T. (2015). *To serve with honor: Doing the right thing in government*. Loftlands Press.

O'Brien, A. (2014, March 26). *Rethinking class ranking*. Edutopia Education Trends: George Lucas Educational Foundation. https://www.edutopia.org/blog/rethinking-class-ranking-anne-obrien

Rose, T. (2016). *The end of average*. HarperCollins.

Sackstein, S. (2015, May 21). *Rethinking honor roll, de-emphasizing academic competition*. Education Week. https://www.edweek.org/leadership/opinion-rethinking-honor-roll-de-emphasizing-academic-competition/2015/05

Shatz, I. (n.d.). *The backfire effect: Why facts don't always change minds*. Effectiviology. https://effectiviology.com/backfire-effect-facts-dont-change-minds/

Tennessee Higher Education Commission.(2012). *A comparison of states' lottery scholarship programs*. Policy, Planning, and Research Division of the Tennessee Higher Education Commission. https://thec.ppr.tn.gov/THECSIS/Lottery/pdfs/SpecialReports/A%20Comparison%20of%20States%27%20Lottery%20Scholarship%20Programs%20120717.pdf

Tribune. (2013, June 5). *School has 29 valedictorians? Is that too many?* [Video file]. https://news.yahoo.com/video/school-29-valedictorians-too-many-121029330.html

Tyner, A. (2021, August). *How to sell SEL: Parents and the politics of social-emotional learning*. Fordham Institute. https://sel.fordhaminstitute.org/

Valedictorians: Who needs them? (2012, July 3). Editorial. *Los Angeles Times*. http://articles.latimes.com/2012/jul/03/opinion/la-ed-valedictorian-20120703

Wormeli, R. (2010, February). *Honor roll? Really?* Association for Middle Level Education. https://www.amle.org/honor-roll-really/

CHAPTER 8

....

FOCUS ON
A REPORTING SYSTEM

Report cards will always be an essential component in grading and reporting. Yet despite their importance, report cards represent only one of the many ways educators communicate with parents and families. Reform efforts that focus solely on revising the report card report generally yield only modest results because they neglect the many other important means of communicating information about students' performance in school (Guskey, 2009).

Successful reform leaders and teachers take a more holistic approach and consider an entire *reporting system*. Such a system includes all the different means available to educators for sharing information about students' learning progress (see Guskey & Bailey, 2001). In this chapter we explore these different ways of communicating, explain how to take advantage of their positive attributes, describe how to avoid their potential shortcomings, and discuss how to integrate these different communication tools in a meaningful reporting system.

YOU ARE THE MESSAGE

Before turning to specific means for sharing information with parents and families, one crucial aspect of communication needs to be emphasized. We must always keep in mind that the effectiveness of any communication depends not only on the *quality* of the information shared but also on *how* that information is conveyed. In particular, the way school leaders and teachers frame their messages and structure their conversations with parents and families greatly influences how that information will be received, what the reaction will be, and what results are likely to follow.

Parents and families often express fear and apprehension when contacted by educators, primarily because those contacts are usually prompted by some trouble or difficulty their child is experiencing in school. Teachers are much more likely to contact parents and families to help solve a problem than they are to share a success. To overcome these initial concerns, it's best to begin any interaction with parents and families with something positive and supportive.

Above all, parents and families want to know that educators are "on their child's side" (Smith et al., 2023). They want to believe that both school leaders and teachers sincerely care about their child and are doing all they can to ensure their child's well-being and success in school. A sense of caring needs to prevail in every interaction, whether it be a casual conversation, phone call, e-mail message, or formal parent–teacher conference.

> *A sense of caring needs to prevail in every interaction, whether it be a casual conversation, phone call, e-mail message, or formal parent–teacher conference.*

A simple and easy way to convey this sense of caring is to follow a simple four-step process in every form of communication with parents and families (see Guskey, 2019). This process doesn't soften or distort the information to be communicated in any way. It simply ensures that the message will be openly received, appropriately interpreted, and yield positive results for everyone involved.

The four steps educators should follow in *all* interactions and communication with parents and families are these:

1. *Always begin with something positive.* Comments to parents and families—as well as to students—should first point out what the child does well and what successes they have achieved.

2. *Identify what specific aspects of their child's performance need to improve.* Parents and families need to know precisely what difficulties (if any) their child is experiencing so they know how best to target improvement efforts at home.

3. *Offer specific guidance and direction for making improvements.* Parents and families also want guidance from teachers about what steps they can take to help their child improve and better meet the learning expectations for the subject area or class.

4. *Express confidence in their child's ability to succeed.* Perhaps most important, parents and families need to know that teachers and school leaders believe in their child, are on their side, see value in their work, and are confident they can achieve established learning goals.

The following example from *Instructional Feedback* by Jeffrey Smith, Anastasiya Lipnevich, and Thomas Guskey (2023) describes a phone conversation in which the teacher explains a particular student's performance in a high school language arts class, and it illustrates precisely these four points:

> In our recent unit on poetry, David wrote several excellent haiku poems that showed amazing imagination and creativity. A haiku is a traditional Japanese form of poetry that consists of only three lines and usually only 17 syllables, often focusing on images from nature. But he often neglects homework assignments and comes to class unprepared. You might ask him about his homework each evening and ensure he has a quiet place at home to work on preparing for the next day's class. I'm sure if he prepares a bit better, David will do very well in class. (p. 47)

This brief explanation shows that the teacher knows David and is familiar with his work, recognizes what he did well, notes areas for improvement, offers specific suggestions for making those improvements, and expresses confidence that David can learn excellently. Conversations like this not only help parents and families feel good about their child's prospects for success, they also help instill in parents and families a sense of confidence in their child's teacher.

WHEN COMMUNICATING WITH PARENTS AND FAMILIES:

1. Begin with positive comments.
2. Identify the specific aspects of their child's performance that need improvement.
3. Offer specific guidance and direction for making improvements.
4. Express confidence in their child's success.

MEANS OF COMMUNICATING WITH PARENTS AND FAMILIES

Educators have numerous means available for communicating information about students' performance in school to parents and families. Advances in technology have increased the number of communication tools and improved their quality. Described here are several of the means most frequently included in schools' or school districts' reporting systems, the advantages of each, and suggestions on how to use each effectively.

Report Cards

Report cards provide the centerpiece of any grading and reporting system and must be thoughtfully structured. In fact, many parents and families consider the report card the most important document they receive from schools (Newport News Public Schools, n.d.). Report card formats vary and sometimes can be constrained by the computerized grading program employed (see Chapter 4). To be an effective communication tool, however, the purpose of the report card must be clear (Chapter 3) and it must present information in a form that parents and families can easily understand and use to help their child make any needed improvements (Chapter 5; see also Guskey & Bailey, 2010).

MEANS OF COMMUNICATING WITH PARENTS AND FAMILIES

Report cards	Home visits
Notes with report cards	School open houses
Standardized assessment reports	Homework
Weekly/monthly announcements	Evaluated assignments or projects
Phone calls	Portfolios or exhibits
Personal letters	School websites
E-mail messages	Homework hotlines
Text messages	Parent–teacher conferences
Newsletters	Student-led conferences

Notes with Report Cards

Some computerized grading programs allow teachers or school leaders to attach personal notes to students' report cards when posted. These notes often resemble small sticky notes on which teachers can write a brief sentence or two. For example, a teacher might write simply, "Beverly, Great improvement in math! Keep up the good work!" Informal surveys of parents and families reveal these notes are the first thing they read, even before looking at the report card. They always find the notes meaningful and indicate that these special messages help personalize the report card in important ways. Because of their brevity, such notes should *always* be positive, acknowledging improvements or recognizing progress.

Standardized Assessment Reports

In most schools, students are administered standardized assessments on an annual basis as part of statewide or provincial assessment programs. Results from these assessments are generally reported to school leaders and teachers, along with parents and families. Because assessment developers often report results using scales and technical terms that may be unfamiliar to many parents and families, school leaders and teachers need to intervene to ensure that parents and families can make sense of the results. Explaining terms like *stanine*, *percentile*, and *standard score* in language that parents and families understand not only makes the information more meaningful, it also shows that

> Because assessment developers often report results using scales and technical terms that may be unfamiliar to many parents and families, school leaders and teachers need to intervene to ensure that parents and families can make sense of the results.

educators value parents' and families' role and view them as partners in the learning process. Several useful guides are designed to help school leaders and teachers in this process, including *Improving Family and Community Engagement through Sharing Data* by Marion Baldwin and Sally Wade (2012), *Sharing Assessment Results with Parents* by Rachel Brown (2020), and *Tips for Administrators, Teachers, and Families: How to Share Data Effectively*, developed by the Harvard Family Research Project (2013).

Weekly/Monthly Announcements

To keep parents and families informed about what is happening in school and encourage their involvement, many schools use weekly or monthly announcements of upcoming instructional topics or learning goals. Rather than serving as a reporting tool, these announcements apprise parents and families of future assignments and offer suggestions on how to offer support. For example, on the first day of each month, teachers in these schools post a one-page announcement with three sections to all parents and families. The first section explains, "During the next month, these are the major learning goals for our class." The second section describes, "This is what students will be expected to do." And the third section says, "Here are some ways you can help at home." Parents and families know to expect these announcements on the first day of each month and can use them to initiate meaningful conversations with their children about school activities and learning progress.

Phone Calls

Of all the feedback we received through informal surveys of parents and families regarding grading and reporting issues, the most surprising was their perspectives on phone calls. More than 60 percent of the parents and families responding to our surveys reported that they *feared* phone calls from school. When asked why in follow-up interviews, their answers were quite consistent. Most replied that they fear phone calls from school because school officials and teachers typically call for only one of two reasons: My child is in trouble, or my child is sick or hurt. Is it any wonder that parents and families fear phone calls if those are the only reasons they are called?

Many school leaders and teachers are trying to change this by calling home to share good news. Some schools have even established routines whereby teachers call three or four homes each week and always begin the conversation with something positive. For example, they may let parents and families know when a student performed especially well on an assessment or did excellent work on a project or demonstration. But such phone calls needn't be restricted to academic matters only. Other teachers inform parents and families when they observe their child assisting a classmate, intervening to help resolve a conflict, or showing exceptional leadership and responsibility in class.

> *Sharing good news also makes parents more willing to contact teachers and school leaders when home situations might affect students' performance in school.*

A Phone Call Home
bit.ly/3qjkkmb

A school librarian told me about a phone call she made in which a mother was moved to tears upon learning that her daughter had stayed after class without being asked to help restack books and straighten chairs. The mother said the call was the first bright spot in what had been a very difficult week. Sharing good news also makes parents more willing to contact teachers and school leaders when home situations might affect students' performance in school. Rebecca Alber's (2017) article "A Phone Call Home Makes All the Difference" offers valuable suggestions on how to use phone calls to build positive relations between school and home (see the QR code above).

Personal Letters

Personal letters offer an effective way to initiate and sustain communication with parents and families. But like all forms of communication, how the message is communicated is just as important as the message itself.

The best personal letters begin personally, addressing parents or family members by name. Beginning a letter with "Dear Parent or Guardian" gives the appearance of a form letter rather than a personal message addressed to a supportive partner (Indeed Editorial Team, 2023). As we described earlier, be sure to open with good news and keep the tone positive but professional throughout. If asking for something, make sure it is phrased as a polite request or suggestion rather than an order or demand. And always take the time to explain why. Keep the message warm, personable, and respectful. Parents and families want to support all efforts to help their children, but they also want to be treated as partners in the process rather than as uninformed subordinates. Finally, be sure to end with thanks for their continued help and support. The website Priceless Teaching Strategies (see QR code) offers excellent suggestions on crafting helpful letters to parents and families.

> *Parents and families want to support all efforts to help their children, but they also want to be treated as partners in the process rather than as uninformed subordinates.*

Priceless Teaching Strategies
bit.ly/3DDqmRw

Text Messages

Like phone calls, text messages can be a powerful tool in opening pathways of communication with parents and families. They offer the added convenience of allowing parents and families to respond whenever their schedule permits. Furthermore, research shows that text messages from teachers can be effectively used to nudge parents into helping correct learning problems.

A study by Peter Bergman and Eric Chan (2021), for example, used text notifications set up through the computerized grading programs of middle schools and high schools to send weekly alerts to parents and families detailing any missed assignments and absences, not just for each day but for each class. As a result, course failures dropped by 38 percent and class attendance increased by 17 percent among the students whose families got the texts, compared to similar students. An earlier study by Todd Rogers and Avi Feller (2018) yielded similar results.

In another investigation, Matthew Kraft and Shaun Dougherty (2013) explored the effects of daily text messages and phone calls home on students enrolled in a mandatory summer school program. They found this daily teacher–family communication increased the odds of students completing their homework by 40 percent, decreased instances of teachers having to redirect students' attention to the task by 25 percent, and increased class participation rates by 15 percent.

> *Text messages show teachers' awareness of students' positive attributes and demonstrate teachers' genuine concern for students' well-being and success.*

School Text Messages

bit.ly/3qjkkmb

As we discussed with phone calls, text messages should be used to share good news as well as to alert parents and families to problems and difficulties (Blad, 2023; Jordan, 2023). Text messages show teachers' awareness of students' positive attributes and demonstrate teachers' genuine concern for students' well-being and success. Mukundan Sivaraj's (2022) article "School Text Messages to Parents—What You Need to Know" (see QR code) offers valuable suggestions for effective text messaging.

Newsletters

School leaders and teachers typically use newsletters to inform parents and families about school events, upcoming field trips, or open house nights. But well-constructed newsletters can also be used to create conversations and enhance communication between school and home (Jensen, 2006). Research further shows newsletters that are clear, informative, and easy to read significantly increase parents' and families' perceptions of the school's general outreach efforts (McKinney, 2012). Todd Finley (2018) offers several excellent tips for putting together an effective newsletter in his Edutopia article "Launching an Engaging Newsletter" (see QR code).

> *Research further shows newsletters that are clear, informative, and easy to read significantly increase parents' and families' perceptions of the school's general outreach efforts (McKinney, 2012).*

Tips for Newsletter

bit.ly/3QplkzY

Home Visits

When time and resources allow, home visits can be a powerful way to enhance school and home communication. Home visits also offer teachers unique insights into students' homelife, cultural background, and family relations.

Initial home visits often occur before the school year begins and focus on building relationships. Teachers introduce themselves, ask about the family's hopes and dreams for their child, and learn about any special challenges the family faces. They use this meeting to provide a connection to school for parents and families who otherwise might not reach out to teachers. Later meetings can then be used to describe specific learning goals, discuss their child's learning progress, and offer suggestions for home support.

Studies show that home visits can be an especially valuable strategy for helping to reduce student absenteeism. An investigation by Steven Sheldon and Sol Bee Jung (2018) of Johns Hopkins University found that students whose families received at least one visit from teachers a year were 21 percent less likely to be chronically absent than other students. What's more, the impact extended to the entire school when 10 percent or more of students had home visits. Helpful suggestions for conducting effective home visits can be found at Parent Teacher Home Visits (PTHV), Project Appleseed, and Learning for Justice (see QR codes at right).

Parent Teacher Home Visits
https://pthvp.org/

Project Appleseed
bit.ly/3DGOm6E

Learning for Justice
bit.ly/3OrtghA

SCHOOL OPEN HOUSES

School open houses are usually evening events that allow parents and families to visit their child's school and meet their child's teachers. Open house meetings held at the beginning of the school year serve mostly to acquaint parents and families with school routines and classroom procedures, although some teachers use the occasion to describe upcoming assignments, class projects, or special events such as field trips. Later in the year, open house meetings allow parents and families to meet with teachers to discuss issues related to their child's learning progress, areas of strength, and areas where additional

STOP AND REFLECT

- For teachers: Think about a student (present or past) who either missed turning in assignments and/or was chronically absent. Which of the modes of communication described above would be most effective for communicating with the parent of this child? Keeping in mind the theme of opening your communication with a positive message, what would be the content of your communication?

- For school leaders: How might you launch and sustain a home visit initiative with your staff? What are some potential barriers you might encounter? How can you and your staff work toward removing these barriers?

time and study may be needed. They also provide an opportunity for parents and families to share information about their child's special interests, academic struggles, or family situations that might impact school performance.

STOP AND REFLECT

- For teachers and school leaders: How might you accommodate parents who are unable to attend evening meetings because of work schedules or other important priorities?

- For teachers and school leaders: How might you work to communicate with parents who are not English speakers?

In some schools, students accompany their parents and families to open houses meetings, lead them on tours of the school and classroom, describe daily routines, and explain activities and projects in which they are involved. In many elementary schools, students prepare their classrooms for open house meetings by decorating the room and displaying artwork, science projects, and other assignments. To encourage participation, some schools provide bus service to open house meetings for parents and families who may not have available transportation. This also allows parents and families to gain a better understanding of the average school day through the eyes of their child. Great ideas for organizing successful school open houses are available from EducationWorld and Teachmint (see QR codes at right).

Education World
bit.ly/43O2mWx)

Teachmint
bit.ly/3QhKv7s

Homework and Evaluated Assignments or Projects

Although the research on parents' and families' involvement in homework shows generally positive effects, results vary greatly depending on the grade level of the students, the subject area of the assignment, and the nature of involvement (see Patall et al., 2008). Yael Grinshtain and Gal Harpaz (2021) identified three forms of parents' and families' involvement with homework:

1. Parents as reminders

2. Parents as partners

3. Parents as students

Across all forms, however, quality appears more important than quantity. Overall, the best parent and family involvement is aware, prompting, and supportive, but not leading or managing. Research by Sandra Moroni and her colleagues (2015) confirmed "it is necessary to look at how parents help with homework instead of how often they get involved in the homework process" (p. 420), and some parents invest long hours in helping their child in nonproductive ways.

> *Overall, the best parent and family involvement is aware, prompting, and supportive, but not leading or managing.*

Aside from their involvement, homework and evaluated assignments or projects can serve as an important source of information for parents and families, showing them the learning tasks in which students are involved, performance goals associated with those tasks, and their child's learning progress. When evaluated assignments and projects are accompanied by teachers'

> *When evaluated assignments and projects are accompanied by teachers' scoring criteria, they become especially useful in helping parents and families understand performance expectations and how to guide their child in making improvements.*

Homework Guide by Peg Dawson
bit.ly/44OxhDu

Homework Tips From Grace Chen
bit.ly/3Yml4ma

To serve as a valuable communication tool between educators and parents and families, however, portfolios and exhibits must be accompanied by the rubrics teachers use to provide students with feedback on their learning progress and to evaluate their final performance (Brookhart, 2013).

Best Practices for Student Portfolios
bit.ly/3Ok9Aft

scoring criteria, they become especially useful in helping parents and families understand performance expectations and how to guide their child in making improvements. Useful guides for parents' and families' involvement in homework and reviewing evaluated assignments are offered by Peg Dawson of the National Association of School Psychologists and Grace Chen of Public School Review (see QR codes at left).

Portfolios or Exhibits

Like assignments and projects, portfolios and exhibits of students' work help teachers assess higher-level performance goals that require students to apply or transfer what they have learned in new contexts, analyze real-world problems, or synthesize perspectives on complex issues (Calfee & Perfumo, 1993; Ocak & Ula, 2009). To serve as a valuable communication tool between educators and parents and families, however, portfolios and exhibits must be accompanied by the rubrics teachers use to provide students with feedback on their learning progress and to evaluate their final performance (Brookhart, 2013). A clear and concise rubric helps parents and families ensure the guidance and support they offer aligns with teachers' expectations. An excellent review of best practices for using student portfolios to guide students' learning is offered in the EducationWorld review of Kathleen Lundy's (2004) work (see QR code at left).

School Websites

Although school websites vary widely in their quality, detail, and ease of navigation, they can be a valuable source of information for parents and families. Research on school websites reveals, however, that the expectations most websites communicate for parent and family involvement are based mainly on the social aspects of student development rather than on academic or pedagogical issues (Gu, 2017; Taddeo & Barnes, 2016). In this context, school websites provide important information on school schedules and events, staff member and contact information, and school policies and programs. Great ideas for developing more effective and informative school websites that engage parents and families as partners in students' academic development can be found in Finalsite's "What Makes a Good School Website?" and Dorit Tubin and Sarit Klein's (2007) article "Designing a School Website: Contents, Structure, and Responsiveness" (see QR codes at right).

Homework Hotlines

Homework hotlines are typically developed by school districts to provide telephone-based academic assistance to students on homework assignments and related academic tasks. Staffed by experienced teachers and tutors who are paid for their service, most homework hotlines are available from immediately after school until early evening, and many offer services in several languages. Although designed to serve all students, evidence indicates that students from economically disadvantaged backgrounds with limited available resources at home contact homework hotlines more frequently (Kennerly et al., 2011). Kelle Reach and Harris Cooper's (2004) article "Homework Hotlines: Recommendations for Successful Practice" offers excellent research-based guidelines for developing effective homework hotline programs (see QR code above).

The expectations most websites communicate for parent and family involvement are based mainly on the social aspects of student development rather than on academic or pedagogical issues (Gu, 2017; Taddeo & Barnes, 2016).

"What Makes a Good School Website?"
bit.ly/3Qk5IO7

"Designing a School Website"
bit.ly/43X0c74

"Homework Hotlines"
bit.ly/3QFLbDZ

Parent–Teacher Conferences

Parent–teacher conferences are the most common and longest-used form of direct communication between parents, families, and teachers (Coulter, 1947). When well organized, they afford parents and families the opportunity to discuss with teachers all matters related to students' academic progress and behavior in school. Research indicates, however, that teachers are seldom taught how to organize conferences and they, along with parents and families, often find these encounters stressful and ineffective (Lemmer, 2012; Rotter et al., 1987).

STOP AND REFLECT

- For those who are or have been parents of school-aged children, what have been your experiences with parent–teacher conferences? How might the conferences you attended have been improved?

- For teachers: Reflect on a parent–teacher conference in which you participated that didn't go well. What made it stressful? In hindsight, what might you have done differently?

- For school leaders: How might you work with your staff in the interest of providing more effective parent–teacher conferences in the manner of a partnership?

In the book *Instructional Feedback*, Jeffrey Smith, Ana Lipnevich, and Thomas Guskey (2023) offer excellent guidelines for developing a true partnership orientation in parent–teacher conferences and making them a more valuable experience for parents, families, and teachers. They describe the following steps:

1. *Be ready for all your conferences.* Have materials organized and ready to go. Allow enough time, but not too much time.

2. *Be welcoming.* Provide chairs and maybe a note on the door to knock when parents arrive.

3. *Know who's coming to see you.* Do you need a translator, either for a spoken language or for ASL (American Sign Language)? Are there accessibility issues?

4. *Have a place for the conference to occur* with chairs that are usable for bigger people and where you can sit at a round table or on the same side of a table.

5. *Start positive.* Let parents know that you know their child and have their child's best interests at heart.

6. *Let parents know what you are currently working on and what the goals are.* Avoid educational jargon or, if needed, explain any terms they may not know.

7. *Describe how their child is doing.* Outline both strengths and weaknesses. Be prepared to show examples to illustrate your points. Avoid making comparisons to other children in the class, even indirectly.

8. *Talk about upcoming lessons and learning goals,* what their child is working on, and how they can help.

9. *Ask parents* if they have questions.

10. *Really listen.* Parents may know best, after all.

11. *Conclude* with how you are going to stay in touch.

Additional recommendations are provided in Emelina Minero's (2018) article "5 Strategies for a Successful Parent–Teacher Conference" and Linda Starr's (2017) article "Meeting the Parents—Making the Most of Parent–Teacher Conferences" (see QR codes at right). Specific recommendations for parents and families in preparing for parent–teacher conferences are outlined in Andrea Canter's (2023) article "Teacher Conferences—A Guide for Parents" (see QR code).

"5 Strategies for a Successful Parent–Teacher Conference"
bit.ly/3QiD4Ni

Meeting the Parents
bit.ly/3rZ2TrK

Student-Led Conferences

Student-led conferences are one of the fastest growing and most effective ways to enhance communication between school and home (Hackmann, 1996; Kinney et al., 2000). They involve students accompanying their parents or family members to school, explaining in their own words the ideas and concepts they are learning, and showing examples of their work. The teacher serves as a facilitator, assisting students when needed and answering any questions parents or families may have.

"Teacher Conferences –A Guide for Parents"
bit.ly/44UMnYm

Schools that have implemented student-led conferences find they do require significantly more preparation time. Teachers must create a timeline for gathering materials and helping students develop portfolios of their work,

> *When student-led conferences are coupled with the use of portfolios, students assume more responsibility for their learning and see connections between their learning in and outside of school (Conderman et al., 2000; Hackmann, 1996).*

provide opportunities for student reflection on their learning, and prepare notifications and schedules for parents and families (Benson & Barnett, 2005). But studies show this extra time yields important benefits. When student-led conferences are coupled with the use of portfolios, students assume more responsibility for their learning and see connections between their learning in and outside of school (Conderman et al., 2000; Hackmann, 1996). Practical strategies for developing an effective program of student-led conferences are described in Jane Bailey and Thomas Guskey's (2001) book *Implementing Student-Led Conferences* and in Beth Brodie's (2014) article, "Student-Led Conferences: Personalization in Practice."

SUMMARY

Engaging parents and families as true partners in efforts to help their children succeed in school involves more than simply developing a new and improved report card. It requires school leaders and teachers to consider an entire reporting system that includes all the different means of communicating, sharing, and exchanging information between school and home.

School leaders and teachers must be aware of the information needs of parents and families and recognize that how they communicate that information is just as important as the quality of the information itself. They need to ensure the information they provide is sufficiently detailed to guide parents and families in providing appropriate home support, but not so complex that it overwhelms or frustrates them in their efforts to align their support with teachers' expectations. Most important, school leaders and teachers must recognize that effective communication is a two-way process that involves treating parents and families as true partners in efforts to help students learn rather than as simply clients awaiting directions from a higher source.

> *School leaders and teachers must recognize that effective communication is a two-way process that involves treating parents and families as true partners in efforts to help students learn rather than as simply clients awaiting directions from a higher source.*

Successful grading and reporting reforms require school leaders and teachers to take a holistic approach and to consider an entire *reporting system*. Each of the communication means in that system has distinct advantages and specific shortcomings. By combining these means, capitalizing on the positive elements of each while recognizing noted limitations, school leaders and teachers can develop an integrated reporting system for sharing information about students' learning progress in school that offers numerous benefits for students and wins the support of parents and families.

CONCLUSION

Gaining the support of parents and families for grading reforms is not an insurmountable challenge. But it's also not a process that can occur without purposeful planning and thoughtful effort.

The school leaders and teachers most likely to succeed in grading reforms are those who understand the change process, initiate reform efforts by clarifying the purpose of grading, make effective use of computerized grading programs, keep the report card simple and family friendly, replace old grading traditions with new and better traditions, and focus on a reporting system. These crucial steps will help them to develop real partnerships with parents and families based on reciprocal relationships and shared responsibilities.

> *The school leaders and teachers most likely to succeed in grading reforms are those who understand the change process, initiate reform efforts by clarifying the purpose of grading, make effective use of computerized grading programs, keep the report card simple and family friendly, replace old grading traditions with new and better traditions, and focus on a reporting system.*

Grading reform efforts built on mutual understanding, reciprocal respect, and shared concern for doing what is best for students are bound to succeed. If the ideas described in this book help you develop that understanding, respect, and shared concern, then it will have succeeded as well.

REFERENCES

Alber, R. (2017, August 25). *A phone call home makes all the difference.* Edutopia. https://www.edutopia.org/article/phone-call-home-makes-all-difference/

Bailey, J. M., &Guskey, T. R. (2001). *Implementing student-led conferences.* Corwin Press.

Baldwin, M., & Wade, S. M. (2012). *Improving family and community engagement through sharing data.* Briefing Paper. https://sedl.org/secc/resources/briefs/improve_family_commun_share/ImprovingFamcommunity.pdf

Benson, B. P., & Barnett, S. P. (2005). *Student-led conferencing using showcase portfolios* (2nd ed.). Corwin Press.

Bergman, P., & Chan, E. W. (2021). Leveraging parents through low-cost technology: The impact of high-frequency information on student achievement. *Journal of Human Resources*, 56(1), 125–158.

Blad, E. (2023, May 16). *These factors are linked to high school attendance. Does your school have them?* Education Week. https://www.edweek.org/leadership/these-factors-are-linked-to-high-student-attendance-does-your-school-have-them/2023/05?utm_source=nl&utm_medium=eml&utm_campaign=eu&M=6845100&UUID=a4b7c2132d-d8ee008ebd97b30c19b50e&T=9155509

Brodie, B. (2014). Student-led conferences: Personalization in practice. *Principal Leadership*, 15(1), 34+.

Brookhart, S. M. (2013). *How to create and use rubrics for formative assessment and grading.* Association for Supervision and Curriculum Development.

Brown, R. (2020, January 25). *Sharing assessment results with parents.* Illuminate Education. https://www.illuminateed.com/blog/2020/01/sharing-assessment-results-with-parents-families/

Calfee, R. C., & Perfumo, P. (1993). Student portfolios: Opportunities for a revolution in assessment. *Journal of Reading*, 36(7), 532–537.

Canter, A. (2023, January 31). *Teacher conferences—A guide for parents.* Child Mind Institute. https://childmind.org/article/teacher-conferences-a-guide-for-parents/

Conderman, G., Ikan, P. A., & Hatcher, R. E. (2000).Student-led conferences in inclusive settings. *Intervention in School and Clinic*, 36(1), 22–26.

Coulter, K. C. (1947). Parent–teacher conferences. *Elementary School Journal*, 47(7), 385–390.

Finley, T. (2018, May 4). *Launching an engaging newsletter.* Edutopia. https://www.edutopia.org/article/launching-engaging-newsletter/

Grinshtain, Y., & Harpaz, G. (2021). Whose homework is it? Different types of parents' dependent help-giving in homework. *Elementary School Journal*, 122(2), 233–256.

Gu, L. (2017). Using school websites for home–school communication and parental involvement? *Nordic Journal of Studies in Educational Policy*, 3(2), 133–143.

Guskey, T. R. (2009). Grading policies that work against standards...and how to fix them. In T. R. Guskey (Ed.), *Practical solutions for serious problems in standards-based grading* (pp. 9–26). Corwin Press.

Guskey, T. R. (2019). Grades versus comments: Research on student feedback. *Phi Delta Kappan*, 101(3), 42–47. https://www.kappanonline.org/grades-versus-comments-research-student-feedback-guskey/

Guskey, T. R., & Bailey, J. M. (2001). *Developing grading and reporting systems for student learning.* Corwin Press.

Guskey, T. R., & Bailey, J. M. (2010). *Developing standards-based report cards.* Corwin Press.

Hackmann, D. G. (1996). Student-led conferences at the middle level: Promoting student responsibility. *NASSP Bulletin*, 80(578), 31–36.

Harvard Family Research Project. (2013). *Tips for administrators, teachers, and families: How to share data effectively.* http://www.hfrp.org/var/hfrp/storage/fckeditor/File/7-DataSharingTipSheets-HarvardFamilyResearchProject.pdf

Indeed Editorial Team. (2023, April 14). *Best examples of teacher introduction letters to parents.* https://www.indeed.com/career-advice/starting-new-job/letter-of-introduction-for-teacher

Jensen, D. A. (2006). Using newsletters to create home-school connections. *The Reading Teacher*, 60(2), 186–190.

Jordan, P. (2023). Attendance playbook: Smart strategies for reducing student absenteeism post-pandemic. *FutureEd & Attendance Works.* https://www.future-ed.org/wp-content/uploads/2023/05/Attendance-Playbook.5.23.pdf

Kennerly, B., Menard, A., & Witty, G. (2011). *Homework hotline: Toward realizing the full potential*. Vanderbilt University Capstone. https://ir.vanderbilt.edu/bitstream/handle/1803/5197/Capstone%20Kennerly%20Menard%20Witty%202011.pdf?sequence=1&isAllowed=y

Kinney, P., Munroe, M. B., & Sessions, P. (2000). *A school-wide approach to student-led conferences: A practitioner's guide*. National Middle School Association.

Kraft, M. A., & Dougherty, S. M. (2013). The effect of teacher–family communication on student engagement: Evidence from a randomized field experiment. *Journal of Research on Educational Effectiveness, 6*(3), 199–222.

Lemmer, E. M. (2012). Who's doing the talking? Teacher and parent experiences of parent–teacher conferences. *South African Journal of Education, 32*(1), 83–96.

Lundy, K. G. (2004). *What do I do about the kid who...?: 50 ways to turn teaching into learning*. Pembroke Publishers.

McKinney, J. B. (2012). *The evaluation of the effects of school newsletters on parent perceptions in an urban school system* [Unpublished doctoral dissertation] Temple University, Philadelphia, PA. https://scholarshare.temple.edu/handle/20.500.12613/758

Minero, E. (2018, October 5). *5 strategies for a successful parent–teacher conference*. Edutopia. https://www.edutopia.org/article/5-strategies-successful-parent-teacher-conference/

Moroni, S., Dumont, H., Trautwein, U., Niggli, A., & Baeriswyl, F. (2015). The need to distinguish between quantity and quality in research on parental involvement: The example of parental help with homework. *Journal of Educational Research, 108*(5), 417–431.

Newport News Public Schools. (n.d.). *Report cards*. https://sbo.nn.k12.va.us/curriculum/staff development/report_cards.pdf

Ocak, G., & Ula, M. (2009). The views of students, teachers, and parents and the use of portfolio at the primary level. *Procedia—Social and Behavioral Sciences, 1*(1), 28–36.

Patall, E. A., Cooper, H., & Robinson, J. C. (2008). Parent involvement in homework: A research synthesis. *Review of Educational Research, 78*(4), 1039–1101.

Reach, K., & Cooper, H. (2004). Homework hotlines: Recommendations for successful practice. *Theory Into Practice, 43*(3), 234–241.

Rogers, T., & Feller, A. (2018). Reducing student absences at scale by targeting parents' misbeliefs. *Nature Human Behaviour*. https://scholar.harvard.edu/files/todd_rogers/files/rogers_sdp_-_final.pdf

Rotter, J. C., Robinson, E. H., & Fey, M. A. (1987) *Parent–teacher conferencing—What research says to the teacher* (2nd ed.). National Education Association.

Sheldon, S. B., & Jung, L. B. (2018). *Student outcomes and parent teacher home visits*. Center on School, Family, & Community Partnerships, Johns Hopkins University. https://pthvp.org/wp-content/uploads/2022/03/student-outcomes-and-parent-teacher-home-visits.pdf

Sivaraj, M. (2022, June 28). *School text messages to parents—What you need to know*. CallHub. https://callhub.io/school-text-messages-to-parents/

Smith, J. K., Lipnevich, A. A., & Guskey, T. R. (2023). *Instructional feedback: The power, the promise, the practice*. Corwin Press.

Starr, L. (2017, February 3). *Meeting the parents—Making the most of parent–teacher conferences*. Education World. https://www.educationworld.com/a_curr/curr291.shtml

Taddeo, C., & Barnes, A. (2016). The school website: Facilitating communication engagement and learning. *British Journal of Educational Technology, 47*(2), 421–436.

Tubin, D., & Klein, S. (2007). Designing a school website: Contents, structure, and responsiveness. *Planning and Changing, 38*(3–4), 191–207.

INDEX

A SAGE Publishing Company

Helping educators make the greatest impact

CORWIN HAS ONE MISSION: to enhance education through intentional professional learning.

We build long-term relationships with our authors, educators, clients, and associations who partner with us to develop and continuously improve the best evidence-based practices that establish and support lifelong learning.

Additional support for educators working to turn parents into trusted partners.

Educators seeking to transform outdated grading practices often struggle to gain the support of students' families. Happily, some are finding ways to engage parents and families as trusted partners in grading-reform efforts. We want to learn about your grading-reform efforts and the successes you've achieved. Furthermore, if problems or concerns arise, we hope you won't hesitate to contact us. Please reach out to share your experiences and questions as you begin this important work of making grading more accurate, meaningful, and equitable.

ABOUT **THOMAS R. GUSKEY**

Thomas R. Guskey, PhD, is professor emeritus in the College of Education at the University of Kentucky. He began his career in education as a middle school teacher and later served as an administrator in Chicago Public Schools. He earned his doctoral degree at the University of Chicago under the direction of Professor Benjamin S. Bloom. What makes him unique as an educational consultant is that his work has been honored by both researchers and practitioners alike. He was named a Fellow in the American Educational Research Association and was awarded the association's prestigious Relating Research to Practice Award. He was also awarded Learning Forward's Outstanding Contribution to the Field Award and Phi Delta Kappa's Distinguished Educator Award.

For help with questions or concerns regarding Mastery Learning, or for virtual or in-person consulting, **contact Thomas R. Guskey by email at guskey@uky.edu, X at @tguskey, or at www.tguskey.com.**